Scottish F... ...n project
run by Scottish Book Tru... ...ok Trust
invited people all over S....... .. write stories and share their
family stories about a special family member or a story that had
been passed down through generations. This book contains a
selection of the best stories from members of the public and well-

Scottish Family Legends

Luath Press Limited

EDINBURGH

www.luath.co.uk

First Published 2011

in association with Scottish Book Trust

Scottish Book Trust is grateful for the generous support
of Heritage Lottery Fund.

ISBN 978-1-906817-93-0

The paper used in this book is neutral sized and recyclable. It is
made from elemental chlorine free pulps produced in a low-energy,
low-emissions manner from renewable forests.

Printed and bound by
CPI Bookmarque, Croydon CR0 4TD

Typeset in 10 point Sabon
by 3btype.com

Cover design by Stewart Bremner, photos by Chris Scott

Contents

CONTENTS

ACKNOWLEDGEMENTS

SCOTTISH BOOK TRUST would like to thank the following people for their help and enthusiasm in making the Family Legends project so successful and in turn making this book possible.

Audrey Dunn and the staff at Heritage Lottery Fund in Scotland, Jane Fowler, Carolyn Becket and Serena Field at BBC Radio Scotland, Jelica Gavrilovic, Uuganaa Ramsay, Kirstin Fairnie, Amanda Block, Yvonne McLean, Merlyn Riggs, Helen Caldwell, Megan Primrose, Al Innes, Francesca Brennan, Chris Scott, Alan Bissett, Mae Stewart, Willie Robertson, Robert Douglas, Stuart Donald, Bernard MacLaverty, Nick Rougvie, Bill Whiteford, Sarah Smith, Nancy Somerville, Alan Addison, Matthew Pearce, Rachel Hosker and the staff at the Hawick Heritage Hub, Alison Murgatroyd, Amina Shah, Jane Shirra, Eddie Kelly, the staff of Clydebank Library, the staff of The Mitchell Library, Marion Lawton and the staff at The National Museum of Rural Life, Cameron Rickards, Leila Cruikshank, Stewart Bremner, all the teachers and tutors who encouraged their students to take part and everyone who wrote and shared their stories throughout the project.

Introduction

EVERYONE HAS A relative whose stories are passed on from one generation to the next – a legend in their own right. They might be a great uncle renowned for their bravery or skill or a granny notorious for her adventures and scrapes. These stories stand up to frequent retelling yet rarely make it outside the family circle.

So we set out to capture the tales that make up our collective heritage. We asked members of the public to send us their family stories and the response was overwhelming. Over 700 people shared their legends on our website or sent them by post.

As the stories poured in, common themes began to emerge: we are proud of our ancestors who fought in wars and have a special fondness for the footballers and cake bakers in our families. A seafaring nation, Scots have travelled the globe and welcomed other cultures into our midst.

Although only a small selection of the stories is presented here, we hope that this book will give you a taste of the diversity of Scottish culture. These stories have touched and inspired us and made us look at our own lives in different ways. We hope that you will enjoy *Scottish Family Legends* as much as we have.

Marc Lambert CEO
Scottish Book Trust

GREAT GREAT UNCLE ALBERT:
A TRUE STORY

Glenn Merrilees

Ma great great Uncle Albert
he used tae hunt fur whales,
way back many moons ago
he telt some right tall tales.

Him and two wee fellas
just bobbin' on the sea,
pulled the whales in pure brute strength
he wis forever tellin' me.

He'd open all thae whales up
wie a knife six inch in length,
'it's no aboot the blade son
it's aw aboot yer strength.'

He'd salt them oan his washing line
a fact he swore wis true,
but did he stretch the truth a bit?
I'll leave that up to you.

He used tae fight thae dinosaurs
when he wis just a lad,
that's how they're awe extinct noo
oor Albert did no bad.

You've heard aboot thae pyramids
architecture wis his pride,
forgot tae pit the windies in
so ye couldnae see ootside.

He hud a pal cawed Noah
they'd play fitbaw in the park,
then he went an goat a joab wi' him
aye they built this muckle Ark.

They started savin' animals
preferably in twos,
they built themselves an awfy set
maistly pilfered fae the zoos.

Then it started bleedin' rainin'
fur forty days and nights,
wee coarner shoap goat flooded
an it grounded loads o' flights.

He built this wall in China
you can see from outer space,
the Chinese awe felt safer
pit the Mongols in their place.

One day he thought gunpowder
long before the great Chinese,
the first explosion in his kitchen
blew aff both his knees!

He said this willnae get me doon
though of course it did a bit,
three inches off his kneecaps noo
and of course he's goat tae sit.

The Great Great fire o' London
it wis him just makin' toast,
it set the hoose oan fire
and loads o' lives were loast.

He said it wis a good thing though
though he wis rather vague,
saved many tens o' thousands
killed off bubonic plague.

Thae rats they hud a killer flea
well so it did transpire,
he wiped oot many millions
by settin' toast oan fire!

He went tae meet King Henry
but arrived there far too late,
instead o' meetin' Henry One
met Henry Number Eight!

So he became an executioner
Anne Boleyn loast her heed,
a wis only dain ma joab son
that's ma only evil deed.

The guy that wrote 'Greensleeves'
said thanks fur stoappin' hassle,
he gave tae him some golden coins
an' gave him this big castle.

Efter that he found America,
Australia, Asia too;
he pit the 'In' in Inca,
he wis the landlord o' Peru.

He wis only fourteen years o' age
when he fought in World War I,
killed oer a hundred Germans
wi two bullets an' one gun.

Penicillin wis another thing
he created in some mugs,
doctors use it worldwide noo
tae fight off killer bugs.

He went an built the Forth Rail Brigg,
he done it in a day,
just a hammer an' some copper nails
tae keep the rust away.

Saved Amsterdam fae floodin'
whilst oot there wi' some chums,
saw two holes appearin'
so he stopped them wi his thumbs.

Electricity ther's another thing
he swore he did invent,
came up wi that idea
when lightning struck his tent.

World War II rejoined the army,
wore his medals wi great pride,
it was an upset fur the family though
thae were fae tha other side?!

Another tale he told tae me
swore that this wis not a lie,
two days efter bein' demobbed
he wis asked to be a spy.

MI5 or MI6?
I really can't recall;
took care o' thae communists,
broke doon the Berlin Wall.

The man invented plastic
tae save the world fae tears,
nae mare paintin' cast iron pipes,
this stuff will last fur years.

A mind he swam the Channel
tae France an then straight back,
awe tae save a tenner
he'd bet wi' Uncle Jack.

He built the first computer;
some plastic wires and pipe,
a never fell fur that one though
Lord whit a load o' tripe!

One day he went and climbed the Alps
forgot tae take his rope,
way up oan thae maountains
that's where he met the Pope.

'Did you ever meet the Queen?' I asked.
'Son a' fine well mind the day,
no just at her weddin'
it wis me gave her away.'

He set off for the North Pole
oan some fancy expedition,
knocked oot this big polar bear
that's now oan exhibition.

Climbed Ben Nevis loads o' times,
half an oor wis his best,
took him shy o' four long hoors
tae climb Mount Everest.

He used tae take the ferry
and he always wondered why,
a'm only oan this fur three minutes
so he built the bridge tae Skye.

Height problems wi' the waterways
so he signed this mega deal,
goat himsel' some concrete
an he built the Falkirk Wheel.

A mind awe through ma lifetime
some claims they were absurd,
in awe I'd stand and stare at him
and I'd hang oan every word.

Author Stories

THE DAY DAD CAME BACK

Stuart Donald

''AT'S IT, FINISHED NOW,' announces Dad, on completion of the car repair job we'd been working on all morning, 3 May 1980. It drew to a close not only the fitting of a new exhaust, but yet another Saturday morning, in the garage, trying to re-sell Aberdeen FC to my Dad. But even today, he's having none of it, even though we were favourites to win the league. He is still sulking, still so injured by the league and cup final injustices we'd suffered over recent years. Once again, I can only imagine in my nine-year-old mind what it would be like if that mad Aberdeen fan from the '60s, that I'd only caught glimpses of, would reappear and take me to games.

We tidy up the garage and head to the kitchen. An enormous wholesale tub of Swarfega that any MOT garage would be proud of emerges from the cupboard under the sink for stage one in the post car maintenance clean-up process. Stage two is the Fairy Liquid wash, which results as usual in an argument with Mum about why we always have to grease-up the taps. I get a particular bollocking today when I decide for some reason that it would be a good idea to recycle my Granda's line that women should be thankful that they'd menfolk who could do these sorts of jobs around the house, and greased-up taps were a small price to pay. We eventually set the table for lunch.

'Fit are ye dein' this aifternein?' asks Mum, perusing the fridge with her back to Dad sat at the table. Silence.

'Gordon?' prompts Mum.

'Washin' the car,' says Dad eventually. Mum finally comes to the table, sits down, staring at him.

'I thought you did that jist a couple a' wiks ago.'

'Aye. Bit it's needin' done again,' Dad says unconvincingly, still focusing on his intensely crafted sandwich. Looking back, that was the signal that Dad was on his way back. As he delicately slices up tomatoes, the pieces of which he surveys for evenness, the Dons fan he buried in his subconscious two years ago has re-awakened and is now organising his day. Mum looks at him, trying hard to fathom out why on earth he would impose this task on himself so soon after having done it. Unbeknown to Mum, me and even Dad himself – still in denial – he's once again at the mercy of the triumph of hope over experience. Aberdeen's electric late surge in the league had brought him under the Aberdeen spell again and washing the car was the one sure way of making sure he'd get unbroken access to the football on the radio.

With the radio blaring out from the garage, Dad checks his watch incessantly as we get the car wash underway. He starts on the left-side front wing, while I start on the number plate and then, as Dad moves to the passenger's side door, I take on the left-side head-light... 20 minutes on the clock, Hibs 0, Aberdeen 0; St Mirren 0, Celtic 0, Dad's hands circle at a steady pace, water streaming from the large yellow sponge that he regularly dips into the bucket and slaps back on the body of the car, in a manner that implied it was a time-invested skill he'd acquired. I was impressed.

'Is this how you do it Dad?' I ask, focusing more on trying to recreate the large streams of water flowing from my sponge than actually washing the car.

'Aye,' responds Dad without even looking at what I was doing.

'Look Dad, do it this way.' I show him a new technique I invented on the spot, a backwards and forwards motion rather than a circular one...

'YES!' yelps Dad, the shock causing me to stand up abruptly.

... Steve Archibald scores for Aberdeen, 1–0!

Dad's listening to the game! I immediately drop my off-the-cuff alternative washing techniques just in case they might distract him and start washing like him, following his circular motions. Maybe he was out of his sulk!

... the ball runs free at the back post, Watson must score... and he does!

Another stifled yelp from Dad as Aberdeen go two up. Still the washing continues in silence, only now at a faster pace. Still Aberdeen lead Hibs 2–0, St Mirren and Celtic are level at 0–0. Half-time comes just as we finish the soapy wash. We head to the kitchen for a cup of coffee, Dad taking the radio with him.

... 45 minutes away from becoming the first side outside the Old Firm to win the league championship in 15 years... the Dons on the brink of a first league championship in 25 years... a historic second league championship in Aberdeen's 77-year history...

By the time the second half starts, we are both on our way around the car again, cleaning the wheels, wheel arches, wipers and even the aerial... Aberdeen score again in 67 minutes, causing Dad now to react with a fist in the air. I was sure of it now, he must be back; I hadn't seen him like this for years. And no wonder, our win was guaranteed so all that mattered now was that Celtic failed to beat St Mirren. With 15 minutes to go, sponges, hoses, soapy bubbles, cloths everywhere, Dad had stopped washing, resorting to pacing and smoking nervously round and round inside the garage, still clutching his clean water sponge... 10 minutes... 5 minutes... and then, finally, it happened. Aberdeen were champions.

Down at Easter Road, Fergie is exploding with his now legendry 'man possessed' performance, running, leaping and hugging everyone all over the pitch. Likewise, I run around the tree in the middle of our front lawn for a couple of minutes, hoping that Dad would eventually join in. But he just stood beaming, shaking his head. And that was it. He was back. I knew it.

A P.S. FROM GEORGE

Robert Douglas

A SUNDAY MORNING. Late 2008. The phone rings. Half-eight! Somebody's early.

'Hello?'

'Hello! Is that Robert Douglas?' A woman's voice.

'That's me.'

'Ah, my name is Georgina. I'm calling from New Zealand. I'm George McIntosh's daughter!'

'Jeez-oh!'

She sounds nervous. Knows this is a big surprise. I try to put her at ease.

'Well Georgina. Let me tell you right away, this is wonderful news. When he died, six years ago, I thought, that's the end of him. He wasn't married, had no kids. I am SO glad to find he has a daughter.'

'Well. I decided to try and trace Jock,' she laughs, 'that's what my mother always called him. I didn't know his name was George – no wonder I'm Georgina. They lived together less than two years, so I don't remember him. Haven't even got a photograph of him. Don't know what he looked like...'

'I've got photos of him! A school photo when he was 13. Two in the Royal Marines – 1944, the other, 1948. And nice shots of him in his 70s, living in Reefton, South Island...'

'Oh! That's wonderful. I'm dying to see what he looked like. You've written about him haven't you? It's *Night Song of the Last Tram* isn't it? I'm going to...'

'It's okay, I'll send you one. And copies of the photos. You'll soon know a lot about him, Georgina. He has four chapters. My mother, Janet, was his only sister. She was the eldest. Then came James and Bill. George was the youngest. I absolutely adored him. In 1942, when he was 17, he volunteered for the Royal Marines. Their parents were dead, so he spent his leaves with us. You'll read all about it in the book.'

We talk for ages. I find out Georgina is in her late 40s, married to Ray, has three kids. By the time we say cheerio, my new cousin and I are getting on fine.

I lie back. Imagine that! Uncle George has a daughter. He hasn't gone completely. It'll be so good helping her get to know him...

* * *

I love it when Uncle George comes on leave. He sleeps in my bed chair. That's the only time it's used now. My father is in Italy with the army, so I sleep in the big bed with my mammy. We live in a 'single-end', a one-room house in a Maryhill tenement. Ah! But when Uncle George arrives for a few days oor wee house is transformed. I cannot believe how lucky I am that this movie star, in the uniform of the Royal Marines, is MY uncle. Every night, without fail, he comes back from the pub with a new girl on his arm, and two or three other couples. Two of the guys are in uniform, but they can't compete with Uncle George.

That navy blue uniform is made for him. And the forage cap with its red piping, worn at a gravity-defying angle on his blond, wavy hair. I may only be five, but I'm aware the girls can't take their eyes off him. They watch him take his cap off – one blond lock falls onto his forehead – fold it up and slip it under his epaulette.

A blanket is spread on the table, 'screwtop' bottles of McEwan's Pale Ale are opened, shandies made for the ladies and the cards are dealt. I ALWAYS sit next to Uncle George, the latest girl on the other side. He puts his arm round me, squeezes me close. Everybody looks. 'This is my NUMBER ONE pal!' Is it possible to die from pleasure? Next to Ma, I love Uncle George best in the world! I wish he could be on leave FOR EVER.

May 1944. He's back again. Once more our Glasgow single-end becomes a Hollywood film set. Girls with print frocks, permed hair and bright red lipstick flutter about. I'm gonny be like Uncle George when I grow up. King of the World. In reality, he's just 18. He's learning how to drive landing craft on and off beaches. Says it's great fun.

D-DAY 1944. Two weeks after his 19th birthday, he plies his newly earned trade on the Normandy beaches. It's not like the movies. The noise is horrendous, frightening. Battleships, cruisers, firing salvoes for hours on end. Planes bombing a few hundred yards inland. German shells straddle them, the Luftwaffe strafes them, bullets ping off his thin-skinned craft, send up spumes of spray.

Bodies float past. Bump along the side sometimes. Makes you cringe. Just an hour ago they were fit young men. When they've emptied the troopship, he and his mate, Flanagan, will sail back to England aboard her. It can't come quick enough. It doesn't. Their craft is disabled, they're stranded on the beach. For six weeks.

The Beachmaster – the officer in charge of all movement on the beach – commandeers them to act as 'runners' and general dogs-bodies. It is the start of a protracted nightmare. For the entire six weeks, night and day, they are under long-range shellfire from German guns. But as he will tell his brothers, the worst job is clearing the casualties. Especially the dead. It's not sanitised like in John Wayne's films. Bodies, entrails, brains, limbs, THAT'S what you find on a battlefield. Like a bloody explosion in a butcher's shop! Meat strewn everywhere. He can't do it sober. He and Flanagan take to breaking into abandoned houses. As it's France, there's plenty of cognac to be had. In his own words, 'We stayed pissed for the whole six weeks.' It's the only way he can get through it and the start of a lifelong problem with alcohol. He also finishes up a textbook case of 'the guilt of the survivor'.

* * *

After the war he goes from job to job then, in 1948, rejoins the Marines. He will serve on HMS *Belfast* in Korean waters during that war. This earns him the British AND United Nations Korea medals to go with his World War II ones. Upon discharge he marries Joan, a lass from Rochester. His drinking soon puts paid to that. In 1956 he emigrates to New Zealand.

In 1997 I track him down. He dies in January 2002 aged 76. As his next-of-kin I receive his medals. I frame them and hang them on my wall... until 2008.

George has a daughter and grandchildren. I return them to New Zealand. Georgina now has her father's medals, the photos, my book. But I have the memories...

* * *

I sit beside him at our blanket-covered table until, unable to keep my eyes open any longer, Ma bundles me, unwashed, into the big bed.

I fall asleep to the gentle clink of beer bottles, hushed conversations and soft laughter as young folk try to have some fun in the middle of a rotten war. When I waken in the morning, I'll roll to the edge of the big bed, look over the side and watch my Uncle George as he sleeps in my bed chair.

MY FAMILY LEGENDS
Willie Robertson

ANY PERSON MEETING my grannies for the first time would have come away with a very different impression of each.

'Big' Grandma Brannan was just under five feet tall and robust in her appearance and opinions. She was a fervent socialist and would readily expound her views on any subject when asked, usually even before being asked, and would support them with quotes from her inspiration – Karl Marx.

'Wee' Grandma Robertson's wiry frame barely made it over four feet. She was a committed evangelical Christian and would only give an opinion when pressed. But her views were never expressed as opinions, she just told the simple truth through the words of her saviour – Jesus Christ.

First impressions are very often wrong impressions though, because far from being different, these two women were almost identical.

Both were born in Dundee in 1895. Both endured childhoods of squalor and deprivation in slums that should have been completely unacceptable in one of the richest countries on earth. Both were undernourished, undereducated and undervalued. Both should probably have died in infancy when it cost a week's wages to see a doctor, because big Granny Bella had a weak heart and wee Granny Dolly had rickets. But my mum always told us 'It's no' the size o' the dog in the fight, it's the size o' the fight in the dog', and my grannies were living proof.

Although Bella and Dolly were outwardly just wee dogs with not a lot going for them, each fought her own private battle with such tenacity that she won through in the end. Bella fought on when her brother Eddie went off to defend socialism against fascism in the Spanish Civil War (I've still got his medals), and when her husband Patrick broke his back falling from the slates of a tenement roof he was repairing. Dolly kept going when her brothers Tommy and Sam were killed at the Somme and when her husband Willie died before their son, my dad, was 11.

Big Grannie Brannan was forged from the hardest steel known

to man. Her mum and dad brought their two children to Dundee to escape the poverty of Ireland, and so condemned 12-year-old Bella and 10-year-old Eddie to a future of ear-bleeding noise and choking dust in the jute mills. No wonder she read *Das Kapital* and would never bend her will for anyone. No wonder she idolised Karl Marx and Robert Burns. Wee Grannie Robertson took a different approach, she bent like a willow in the breeze. She went to work in the mills as soon as she was able to walk to the gates, because rickets and deformed legs wouldn't stop her from contributing her pittance to the family budget. You could understand why she thought her best chance of survival was to sway in the hurricane, clinging to the words in the Bible that gave her a reason for carrying on. No wonder she loved Jesus.

I was the only boy in my primary school who knew all the words of songs that started 'Jesus wants me for a sunbeam...' as well as 'The workers' flag is deepest red...'

Both women refused to be overwhelmed by a tidal wave of injustice, poverty and disease in a world where everything seemed to be stacked against them. They were invincible because they had the same four powerful weapons in their armoury. Willpower, family, humour, and a mighty superhuman ally ensured they could never be broken. Their willpower was crafted out of iron and willow. Their family support kept them afloat and their humour was stoic, black and daft. But it was the superhero standing beside them that tipped the balance. Dolly held hands with Jesus right to the end, and Bella stood tall and proud at Karl's side to her last breath.

People think of 'legends' as larger than life heroes doing great deeds beyond what the rest of us could manage. In war, in catastrophe, in the most desperate situations, heroes are those extraordinary people who show the kind of courage and grit we all wish we had. Grannie Robertson and Grannie Brannan weren't larger than life. If anything, they were smaller than life. They were two tiny people grinding on and thinking they were making no real difference in a big unfair world. Eddie, Tommy and Sam could at least hold a rifle to defend freedom, but my grannies were too little. It's hard to take up arms when the rifle is bigger than you.

But they actually changed just about everything. They and their generation won two world wars, brought in the Welfare State and a National Health Service, got women the vote, made sure kids got free education, free milk and free meals. Most importantly, they gave me and my brothers values and a sense of humour that has endured all our lives.

Grannie Robertson and Grannie Brannan shot the status quo to bits without ever touching a gun. So if you want to meet true larger than life legends, don't look to Alexander the Great or Napoleon. Ask about Dolly Robertson and Isabella Brannan.

MEH AUNTIE MARY

Mae Stewart

MY GREAT AUNTIE Mary lived one storey up; in a stair-worn tenement in Dundee; in her pristine wee two-roomed but-an-ben. She lived there most of her life. I remember her saying to me once; 'Eh've pehd rent here a' meh days, an' if Eh stole a bliddy brick Eh could get the jail! Somethin fell wrang there iz thir no'?'

She would've been 148 years of age this year had we discovered a gene to take us past the 100-year mark and beyond. I am certain that if anyone could have made it, she would have still been with us!

Auntie Mary was my father's aunt; my mother's extra mother; and our extra grandmother. She served as family councillor; home baker; one of our main 'helper-ooters'; baby sitter; knitter in chief for us five kids; supplier of school shoes (but never for our Christmas or birthdays); and my mother's dearest friend and confidant.

In her time Auntie Mary had been a suffragette. A lifetime committed socialist, she was amongst the first women shop stewards in the jute mills in Dundee. She started work in the mills at age 10 as a part-time worker. She retired at age 65. She was a strong independent role model, especially for us lassies!

My memories of Auntie Mary began almost from the day my mother carried me over her doorstep; long before I realised that the mind and heart can store such memories. She remained in my life physically until I was 17 years of age, when she died. She has remained in my heart for this past 54 years, and I'm sure will do so for my 'forever'.

Auntie Mary had no children of her own. She nursed her mother and father in that same house until they died, then she just carried on living there. She had many, many friends; and us of course.

We kids visited almost every Sunday afternoon. My eldest sister would take us 'a hurl on the tramcar' for our Sunday jaunt. Auntie Mary had an inside toilet (pretty posh having an inside lavvie in my neck of the woods when I was a kid).

Weather permitting, every week, we (my brother, my sister and I) walked with Auntie Mary to 'visit' our relatives up at the 'Hullie' (Balgay Hill cemetery). There we would change the flowers and wash the head stones. If we complained she would say; 'Niver mind yehr mumpin'! They belang tae us! This is a mark o' respect.'

On the way home we would get an ice cream cone. In winter time it was the same procedure but the ice cream was replaced with a bag of chips to heat us up.

I loved hearing about when she was young and a suffragette. How she would march up Reform Street in Dundee with her banner shouting 'Votes for Women!' She would get up on the horse and cart that the suffragettes parked outside the High School gates, and speak about why women had the right to vote. She told me; 'Wid yeh believe it, fowk, an' no' jist men, yazed tae throw bits o' auld cabbages an' the like at yeh.'

'Oh! Auntie Mary,' says I, 'that must've been jist affy!'

'Well!' she replied. 'Eh could think o' better things Eh wid've liked tae happen tae iz, but Eh jist picked it up an' threw it right back! It took mair than an auld bit cabbage leaf tae shut me up!'

Auntie Mary was mainly self-taught and educated by books from the library. She joined the Labour Party as a young woman. All her working life she joined in the fight for better pay and conditions for mill workers.

My auntie had 'a guid pair o' hands on her'. She could knock up a great pot of 'stand-yehr-spane-in-it' soup.

However, one of my everlasting memories was just how quick she could knit. She fair clickety-clicked away with the needles, and supplied us with anything that could be knitted; school jumpers and socks; fancy jumpers and skirts; dallies' clahes (dolls' clothes); beddies (bedcovers); all our 'new-bairn' stuff, including massive lacy shawls.

She was never off the go. When she saw you she always greeted you as though you were the best thing that was going to happen to her that day. She gave massive cuddles. I wish I was allowed more than a thousand words to tell you all about her; so I could do her justice!

She died, at age 94.

I was helping my mother clear out her flat when we came across two small books.

One was a school jotter. In it were sections on us five kids from the day we were born; details of our birth weight to our first school reports, and so on.

In my mind's eye, I see my mother still; sitting on the end of Auntie Mary's bed in floods of tears, rocking back and forth, cradling that jotter.

Later, we opened what was a wee account book and it was for the grocer's shop just down the road, and there was a written list of money that was paid in each week, then at Christmas time there was a list of groceries far too big to be Auntie Mary's, and there was some money left in the account.

My mother told me that when she enquired at the grocer's, the man informed her that he had been sworn to secrecy by Auntie Mary. She saved some money all year round, and then Christmas week he would make up small parcels for the folk he knew could not afford much, and distributed them saying they'd been donated anonymously.

My mother left him the book, after putting a last 'Auntie Mary' donation in it.

He thanked her, saying, 'Eh think Mary wid've liked that. She wiz a real gem o' a wumin!'

Well he was preaching to the converted telling us that, that's for sure!

Stories from our
Family Legends
Community Ambassadors

GRANNY

Kirstin Fairnie

MY GRANNY WAS the queen of embellishment. In those tender years before the insidious cynicism that came with adolescence, I was one of the few lucky enough be invited in to her world of superlatives, exaggerations and dramatic liberties. Anything was possible, and best of all, all the characters were people I knew.

Granny's enchanted web was spun so adeptly that it wasn't until I came to writing this Legend that it dawned on me that perhaps some of the stories might not be true. But the excitement of never quite knowing where to make the distinction between fact and fiction is what made my granny's story-telling so addictive, and the stories' endurance is testament to my granny's legendary talent for... well, spinning family legends. My father has indeed described her as an early blueprint for Google: a font of much information, little of it wholly reliable.

What better subject for a family legend? Not only was my granny herself a legend, she also created legends.

Perhaps her legendary ability to create a story came from her days as a young journalist working first for D.C. Thomson, and later in London, where she worked for women's magazines, and where she adopted the rich, luxurious tones of the Morningside accent she used throughout the rest of her life.

Working as a journalist in London, she was living her dream. Societal restraints imposed upon women of my granny's generation meant that when she was 26, she was forced to put aside her own dreams and instead cut the figure expected of her as a respectable wife to Andrew, a sales manager for a paper bag manufacturer (who coined the phrase 'treesaver' for eco-paper bags, by the by).

The happiest event of her life also caused one of the greatest disappointments, when her Editor responded to her excited engagement announcement with crushing bluntness: 'That'll be you handing in your notice then.'

Years later, now living in Edinburgh, Granny would use her legendary aptitude for creating stories to develop spurious excuses for going out. Like a horse breaking free, she would dash down to

Waverley Station, where she would await the London–Edinburgh train with gleeful anticipation. When it arrived, she would beam at the strangers from London as they rushed past her, wondering at their cosmopolitan style clashing with the grey, dowdy streets of Edinburgh. As the train pulled away, she would touch it, returning home with a little of the mystery and romance of the British capital rubbed off in the dust on her fingers.

Granny's journalistic career may not have lasted officially for as long as she would have liked, but she put her snout for a good story to good use to spice up family life. Her uncanny ability to be in just the right place at just the right time (handily enough, she was always the sole witness to the most unbelievable of domestic scoops) provided her with ample material to bulk out her tea-time news bulletins.

As a child, I would gaze longingly at the Chanel frocks Granny had acquired during her time on Fleet Street. But the glamorous allure of designer dresses was nothing compared to the hilarious image of my granny stalking the streets of Edinburgh and Glasgow in her home-made cauliflower bunnet. Granny had been commissioned to answer the Scottish version of Douglas Adams' 'Ultimate Question of Life, the Universe, and Everything': who's friendlier Glaswegians or Edinburghers?

Granny rejected Balenciaga for brassica, donned her cauliflower hat, and hit the catwalks of Princes Street and Sauchiehall Street, observing the differing reactions of the inhabitants of Scotland's capital and its largest city. The cries of 'Do you know you've got a cauliflower on your head hen?' made Glasgow the clear winner against the disdainful glances Granny received in the capital.

Granny's unconventional relationship with the brassica family doesn't end there. My mum remembers with something less than fondness the first time she had a meal at my dad's house, prepared by my granny. Keen to make a good impression, Granny had excelled herself, with a culinary vision and inventiveness that makes Heston Blumenthal's creations look tame. Ever keen to impart wisdom upon the younger generation, my granny's version of a 'dining experience' differed just slightly from that of the restaurant profession. My mum's struggle with cabbage and lime jelly was definitely a character-building experience.

In fact, Granny's culinary experimentation was legendary

There is nothing more delicious for a child than imagining their parent being naughty, and I used to squirm with mirthful delight at the legend of The Fish in the Drawer. Once, Dad was at home alone with Granny, struggling valiantly with a large plate of smoked fish, a flavour not designed for the five-year-old palate. Mid-way through the meal, the phone rang, and Granny got up to answer it, leaving Dad in the kitchen, alone but for his inexhaustible mound of fish. He seized his chance. In a flash of brilliance, Dad prised open the heavy drawer under the dining table, and scraped his plate hurriedly into it. Artful arrangements of napkins created the illusion of there being 'nothing to see here'. Returning from the telephone call, Granny was surprised to see Dad's cleaned plate, and his grinning, angelic face above it. It was not until some weeks later, driven wild by the stench of rotting fish percolating throughout the house, that Granny discovered the explanation for Dad's over-the-top appreciation of her fish-cooking skills.

I will never forget the most delicious meal I ever ate at my granny's house: a plate of shepherd's pie. Keen to encourage Granny to try the recipe again, since it seemed she had found her forte with it, I showered her with appreciative 'mmm's and asked for helping after helping. Which in large part contributed to my churning stomach after my granny said to me, 'Oh thank you dear, I'm so glad you liked it. I just thought I'd better use up the mince after eight years in the freezer.'

Granny worked tirelessly for charity throughout her life, and the recipients of her meals on wheels will be pleased to hear she had nothing to do with their preparation! Her love of words and her philanthropic morals helped her to raise extraordinary sums for the annual Christian Aid book sale in her church in Edinburgh. The stories she wrote for me and my sister, illustrated with photographs cut out from old editions of the Reader's Digest, were the most precious gifts we ever received. 'What are you reading?' was always her first question, and this preoccupation with the written word has shaped my own personality. Every time I finish a book now, I wonder what my granny would have thought of it.

MAJKA MOJA MILA – MY DEAREST MOTHER

Jelica Gavrilovic

SHE WAS BORN in 1932 in a village called Kazance tucked away in the mountains between Bosnia and Croatia, youngest of six, there were 30 years between her and her oldest sister. Grandma was 50 years old when she gave birth to my mother – she told her daughter that she never really wanted to have her at such an age, but that she was the best of all her children.

My mother, Milica (Melissa), didn't go to school, although she should have. The war was on and the neighbouring city, Banja Luka, became a Nazi puppet-state for the duration of the war. She would often recall living through World War II as a child and the fear that ran through her. Even as an adult she didn't like the sound of aeroplanes, was afraid of fire and despised fascism. One of her sisters taught her to read Cyrillic, but mostly she learnt to knit, weave, sew and make clothes and look after the farm animals throughout her childhood.

Grandma, who was known for her love of fauna, would always chastise her daughter for not being kind enough to the farm animals. One day she was asked to tend to the bees by her sister, Jela. Milica just didn't have the gift for handling them and soon they set upon her, entangled in her waist-long hair, nipping her scalp, neck and face. She survived of course, but never forgot. She never got on with snakes either and would run as fast as she could to escape angry jumping 'stripeys'.

During World War II, she survived typhoid when she was just nine – all her hair fell away during the fever – disease and chronic illnesses would be spread by visiting armies engaged in guerilla war fare in the forests and mountains. She was also sent to hide high up in the hills many times, along with all the other children, when enemy soldiers passed through the village, crossing from Croatia to Bosnia and back. She would spend days tucked away in bothies dotted about the mountains, tending sheep and goats along with her friends. Mothers and the elders felt it was safer for their children and didn't want to risk them being taken away by the Germans and Croats.

Both her brothers were murdered in a Nazi camp in former Yugoslavia as they were Eastern Orthodox by faith, and along with

Jews and Roma, were considered to be inferior. They fought against the Nazis and their allies for a short time during the war – they were neither pro-royalty or communist. The political history during that time was very complicated. When communism came after the war, life altered for the peasants living in the hills and they lost ownership of their land and were often visited by Yugoslavian militia to be asked to work voluntarily in the cities to rebuild a new country. My mother would return to the tops of the mountains to hide, along with her female friends, to avoid going. She felt it was more important to stay and look after her parents. But eventually things changed and she had to decide whether she was going to stay at home or leave for good.

She was the last at home to look after her parents and came to England in 1962 with just one piece of luggage, to marry my father and to work at Salt's Mill. She weighed a mere seven stone when she arrived – farm work having taken its toll on her body. She was a tall woman. The other mill workers would try to fatten her up with fish and chip suppers from Saltaire chippy, but she stayed skinny for years and years.

My mother was a straight woman, with a dry, laconic sense of humour. She didn't drink alcohol, smoke cigarettes, or eat chocolate. Sometimes she was vilified for speaking her mind – she had no fear of shooting from the hip at any man or woman. She was assertive, with strong opinions on politics and culture and would engage in 'man talk' at the table – she had little time for fish-wife tittle-tattle.

Despite her childhood in war and poverty, she loved her family deeply and was wholly committed to us. She loved completely. She loved children and they knew they were always welcome at our house. During the late 1970s she fed the entire street of kids regularly, all turning up hungry at lunchtimes. They were tough times, but she always found it in her heart to give. For this we loved her too. She made the house welcome to everyone who came by, and sometimes the small living room would be filled with a dozen people chatting away, drinking Turkish coffee and tucking in to gibanica.

She battled with illness all her adult life, and eventually was diagnosed with a terminal cancer which took her away from us after two years of struggling against it. She was stoic throughout, still loving completely. An unforgettable woman: mother, daughter, sister, wife and of course baba.

FAIRYTALE HERO

Uuganaa Ramsay

OUR BABY BILLY with his Celtic red hair and Mongolian blue spots is our family legend. He was a symbol of many nice things. He was the symbol of Mummy and Daddy's love, Scot and Mongol ethnicities, Western and Eastern cultures, Christianity and Buddhism, representing the modern Scotland, modern world. He was only three months old and he hasn't shown anyone his first smiles or looked me in the eye properly since he left us behind. Yet he is our family legend and he will be a legend in many people's minds.

Expecting him to be born and carrying all the dreams and hopes, I bore him just like any baby. From the moment he was born life seemed unfair. The heartbreaking, shocking and devastating news came one after another and tested our strength to the limit.

I'm writing about Billy, announcing to the world how proud I am to be Billy's mummy and he was born to me, to be my son. He was taken away from us because of a tiny extra chromosome. It was a syndrome, it was Down's Syndrome. This tiny chromosome destroyed so much physically and emotionally. But it did not destroy the love of a mother or a father. He was our baby Billy, a baby brother and he will be a big brother and Uncle Billy.

Our baby with golden chest and silver bottom just like the fairytale heroes in Mongolian tales.

All Around the World

THE LONG SHADOW

Joan Lennon

I NEVER MET HIM, my mother's father. He was just stories to me, and not very many of those. My mother barely met him either, since he died of typhus and malaria when she was three. And his wife, my ghastly grandmother (to distinguish her from the nice one) spoke of him and their time in China very little.

Coming of age in the '60s, it was embarrassing being of missionary stock, but I could always say, 'Oh, but my grandfather was a medical missionary.' That made it almost alright.

He went to university straight from the farm, the first of his family. They rushed them through in those days, desperate to get doctors out to the mud and the squalor of World War I. There are a few facts from that time – his attestation papers, for example, tell me he was five foot six inches, with a 33 inch chest (maximum expansion 36 inches,) a good physique and several moles. No stories, though. But as soon as he was home again, he brushed his suit, slicked down his hair and went the rounds of the churches.

'I'm a doctor,' he said. 'Send me to China.'

Well and good, but as each board of church worthies questioned him further, heads would begin to shake. Tutting was distinctly heard. No-one doubted his medical qualifications, but his religion...

It was only on the second round of interviews, after, I expect, some canny coaching, that my grandfather managed to convince the Methodists that he was missionary material.

And then he had to face his mother...

'You're not going without a wife. Take Vera. She's always wanted to be a missionary.'

So he did.

I only picked up a few stories of their time in Szechuan. I know about the time my grandfather's Chinese let him down and the patient he thought he'd told to soak her foot in warm water spent the morning walking up and down on the veranda. I know he liked to relax after surgery by going down to the market and haggling. And, just once, I heard about the habits of his Chinese helper, who longed to be a surgeon too – in charge of the anaesthetic, he would put the patient way, way under, so he could watch my grandfather work. Only the twitching of returning consciousness drove him back to his post. I always liked that helper, though I never knew his name. I wonder what happened to him. I doubt he made old bones. The baron wars were brutal, and he was tarred with the missionary's brush.

But there is one among the few thin images I have of my grandfather that is as clear to me as if I'd been standing right there. It was the time my mother escaped from the house and toddled into the surgery. For me, the scene always includes my grandfather up to his elbows in blood and some poor soul's intestines. And there was my mother, bright-eyed and sturdy, her brown hair all fluffed up and curly in the humid heat, standing in the doorway, cheerfully defiant. In my version of the scene I can see them both, locking eyes across the squalor, oddly equals.

'Go home, Jeanie,' he said.

Apparently, she went.

That's all. Just a snippet – just a glimpse. Not earth-shattering. Set against the impossibly exotic background of Szechuan in the 1920s, it was a peculiarly domestic moment. But I can almost touch it. I know he was proud of her. I know he saw his own relentless spirit in the little girl.

Jeanie was his daughter, all right.

Relative ages can be dizzying. I see my grandfather as a young man, because he was never an old one. I see my mother as a toddler and the old woman she has become in the same breath, as it were. My own sons could stand beside my grandfather as he was then, and though they would tower over him, still to my mind they would make a set, with their youth and energy and desire for what is wide and wild and far away. (Times have changed, of course. As my boys fling themselves away from home to the far-off places of the world I do not insist they pack a wife.)

I never met my grandfather, but in a way, I knew him – know him. He was a short man, with a short life, and all I have are a few snippets of story that live in my mind in a way that facts don't. Just story. But stories can have long shadows.

JOURNEY TO CHINA, 1910

Isobel Mackay

ON SUNDAYS AS A child I was often taken to visit my elderly great Aunt Victoria and great Uncle George, both rather stern people. My mother told me they had been missionaries in China for 30 years.

After my great aunt died, I was given a copy of the diary she kept during her journey to China, aged 24 years, whilst travelling to marry her fiancé George, a medical missionary out there. I was surprised to read she had once been young, adventurous and brave, even had fun...

In October 1910, Victoria arrived at Southampton docks with her parents. Her father had arranged a chaperone, a Miss Smith. Victoria did not want one so planned to avoid her, though she was only going as far as Penang. Safely stowed in the hold was a crate with wedding presents from the family. The ship, a steamer named the SS *Prinz Wilhelm*, set sail at noon. Victoria went below deck for lunch to meet her fellow travellers. They were mostly missionaries, a select lot she thought, some to be avoided.

Afterwards, she located the hurricane deck, saw the wooden steam chairs ready for passengers. By now, the ship was in the Bristol Channel. Victoria felt excited. She knew the journey would take six weeks, south to the Mediterranean, through the Red Sea, down the Suez Canal, sailing east on the Indian Ocean, up the China coast to Shanghai, her final destination, calling at various ports on the way, dropping off passengers.

There was an orchestra on board for dances and fancy dress parties held regularly, also entertainers, including a troupe of Dutch jugglers!

Communal singing took place after dinner, where Victoria often sang solos. Also there was a gymnasium for use in the day time. Some flirtations took place on board between young people. Victoria was engaged so that was not something to indulge in, but all the same became flattered by the attentions of a young man. They spent time walking on deck, talking long and often, but eventually, he had to be given the cold shoulder.

Victoria loved sleeping on deck on warm nights whilst sailing in the tropics. From the deck she admired many beautiful sunsets, sightings of the moon, stars, even a lunar eclipse, lunar rainbow and once, a spectacular thunderstorm on the Indian Ocean.

The ship docked at Colombo and Victoria went ashore, was met by her future in-laws, who took her by pony and trap to lunch at the Hotel Mount Lavinia, where she was presented with several wedding gifts, including the treated skin of a leopard, shot especially for Victoria and George.

Soon after sailing from Colombo, Victoria became violently ill. The ship's doctor dosed her with medicine. Eventually she was carried on deck in a stretcher to be nursed in the fresh air. A week later they reached Singapore. Once passengers disembarked Victoria went to visit the botanical gardens, but soon felt tired due to the heat, returning to the ship early.

Later she received a telegram from home, making her feel emotional. Home seemed a long way away. She still felt rather weak after her illness.

Reaching Hong Kong in late November, again missionaries met the ship, took Victoria by rickshaw up the Peak where she saw marvellous views, similar to the West Highlands in Scotland, she thought, as a mist came down.

Later, on board, Victoria chatted with the remaining passengers for hours, some bound for China, others for Japan, the final port.

The steamer set sail up the East China Sea into stormy weather causing the ship to roll. All Victoria wanted to do was lie on her bunk, or occasionally attempt to pack, not easy on an unsteady ship. Also, she did not have enough luggage, having acquired more belongings in Colombo.

Finally, the ship arrived at Shanghai on the 6th of December, six weeks since leaving Southampton. The passengers taken ashore by tender were met by missionaries, who took Victoria to the mission just in time for Tiffin. Victoria's heart leapt at the welcome sight of a coal fire. She was quite appalled by China. It was overcrowded, bitterly cold as well. She wanted to return home at once. It was a daunting thought to go on, but there was no choice. How she missed the security of the ship!

Besides, Victoria only had four days to make preparations to travel on into the interior of China on two house boats, a journey of five or six weeks.

On the 10th of December, Victoria embarked on a Chinese river boat, the ss *Tuck Woo*, which would sail up the Yangtze river, though she had to change boats halfway. At last, on 28 January 1911, she arrived at Chungking. Missionaries met the boat, welcoming Victoria. She was very glad to be on land, by now rather tired of house boats! It would be months before her fiancé George could join her. The time was spent learning Chinese, preparing for life as a missionary's wife. Sadly, when she opened the box brought from home, all the crockery was smashed, having not survived the boat journey, riding the river rapids. Disappointing, but not a surprise.

Finally George and Victoria were married in October 1911. It was a quiet ceremony, attended by friends. Now her new life could really begin.

MILLA

Franz Grimley

IF YOU THINK OF a legend as being something, or someone, who is still talked about with awe and reverence then my mother, Milla, was such a legend.

She was born in a tiny village just outside the city of Graz, in Austria, and at the age of 18, met and married my father, John Grimley, when he was stationed in Graz at the end of World War II.

I could go on to give you her life story; how she then came to Scotland as a 'war bride' and raised a family of two sons, overcoming the language barrier and the prejudices that were ranged against her but I'd prefer, instead, to give you some idea how she became a legend in our family.

To my kids she was to become known as Granny Milla from an early age. After nearly 25 years of marriage to my father they went their separate ways and Milla returned to her homeland, and Graz. So, to keep her memory alive and fresh in my children's minds we would talk about how their gran lived far, far away. When going for a walk we'd point skywards to a jet contrail and say, 'See, there's Granny in a plane.' So they grew up thinking of their gran as a mysteriously distant relative who they'd meet some day, if they were good.

I'm going to relate just two of the many tales that made Milla stand out from the crowd. The first was told to me by my brother, Ian, who had gone with her to Austria as a 12-year-old and knew of the events first-hand.

During the 1990s, when she was, by then, in her late 60s, Austria was going through a period of political unrest due to the increasing number of immigrants who were passing through its borders and making their homes, and taking all the menial jobs in the cities and towns. As a result of this the ruling party, in order to garner more votes, was considering a policy of re-patriation. Over my mother's dead body. To quote her later, 'They were going to throw out that nice young fellow who sells me my paper in the mornings.' (He was one of those immigrants who stood by at traffic lights and sold newspapers to car drivers as they sat in line.) 'He's never done anyone any harm. It's a shame.' I've no doubt that she remembered from personal experience how difficult it was trying to just get by as an alien in a foreign country. So, what could she do about it? I reckon that most people would do nothing. They'd mump and moan a bit, then accept the decision as inevitable. Not Milla.

'If you're going to complain, go to the top.' She called the Prime Minister of Austria. She, quite literally, picked up the telephone and by some miracle, got straight through to his office. An aide or private secretary answered the phone and asked who was calling and my mother told the gentleman who she was and that she wanted to speak with the Prime Minister. 'Hold on, I'll put you through.'

Sure enough, on the end of the line was the man himself. He listened quietly and patiently as Milla verbally chastised him and his party for being so cruel and heartless. Eventually, he replied in conciliatory tones and said, 'I take your point Mrs Grimley, but I feel I must mention something... you do realise that I'm currently in Cyprus?'

My mother, urgently calculating what the telephone call must be costing her, let out a shriek and slammed down the phone. That was typical of her though. Standing up for the downtrodden.

My second tale relates to a journey I was about to undertake on behalf of the company I used to work for. I was due to travel to Romania, by air of course, and the flight itinerary happened to mention that we would be stopping for a very short period at Vienna Airport before continuing onwards to Timisoara in Romania. I had asked my then boss if it were possible to spend an overnight stop whilst in Vienna and, possibly, meet my mother at some pre-arranged meeting place, but he'd have none of it. I thought long and hard before calling Milla and telling her about this journey. I knew she'd try to travel up from Graz and see me even for those brief minutes but, to me, the brief stop-over wasn't worth her effort. She was getting on in years and the road trip was the best part of 200 miles. I tried to explain to her over the phone that it wasn't worth her while. I'd only be there, in Vienna, for about 20 minutes.

I didn't reckon on a mother's determination to see her son.

We were flying at approximately 25,000 feet on the glide path into Vienna Airport when the pilot made an announcement. 'Would Mister Grimley please make himself known to the cabin staff?'

I gingerly, and with puzzled embarrassment put up my hand.

An air hostess came to my seat and explained that, somehow, my mother had contacted the airport, who then contacted the aircraft, to say that she was going to meet me at Vienna Airport and that all departments in the airport had been put on standby to let me through immigration control, direct me through the building and lead me outside into the main concourse where she would be waiting. And it all happened just like that. The aircraft taxied to a halt, I was first in line to disembark where a whole series of people with smiling faces pointed to where I had to go. It took me about five minutes to arrive where my mother and brother stood behind a small barrier to greet me. Ten minutes later, I was back on board and the plane was preparing for take-off.

That was the legend that was Milla.

HELLO, HELLO, ROBINSON LAKE CALLING

A. Sutherland

'AT LAST I THINK I've really fallen on my feet!' wrote Uncle Jim.

It was 1939 and he was in South Africa where he had recently landed the job of Superintendent of Robinson Lake, a popular resort for the white townsfolk of the Transvaal Witwatersrand gold mines.

'What the hell more can a chap wish for? They don't call me Lucky Jim for nothing!'

A year later my brother Doug and I, then aged ten and eight, were evacuated to Robinson Lake to spend five unforgettable World War II years with Uncle Jim, Auntie Milly and our South African cousins Joan, Jean and Jimmy, aged fourteen, ten and six.

Uncle Jim sent lengthy action-packed progress reports to our anxious suburban parents back in Cardiff. The perfect uncle, who we were so lucky to have known and loved in his prime, leaps from his lively, close-typed, often hand-illustrated, foolscap pages.

'Dear old Bill' ... 'With love from we seven'.

He really liked children, and especially liked having another two in his family.

'Bill the pleasure is ours, and you can guess that I will do everything possible for their comfort and welfare. Most of the supervision will be in the hands of my wife (thank God, sez you?)'

'Al and Doug are in the pink, fit as fiddles, happy and enjoying everything. When asked if they'd like to go back to Cardiff again, the reply is that they have no intention of going back.'

'Your two fit so well in with my three that I'm sure Mill and I forget that they're not our own kids and we'll be pretty heart-broken when the time comes for them to leave us.'

Sport and fitness were the top priorities:

'I started your youngsters on swimming lessons right away. Doug has gone across the lake with me already, a matter of 650 yards; he dives from the five and ten foot boards and is now tackling the 15 foot platform.'

'All our (he later slips in to 'my') kids' swimming has come on a lot and if they keep it up they should do wonders next season. Next year they must all take up life-saving. Doug and Jimmy must get in to water polo and also take their diving more seriously.'

'The (swimming club) Junior Championships were the most important events, and I can tell you it gave me one of my biggest thrills to see your two win on both sections.'

On a big inter-school gala:

'Joan won all the events she went in for... Doug excelled himself in the diving competition...'

'All the kids have been running wild here. They caught 55 fish and cooked them for their supper.'

'Bathing parades at 6 am; another in the afternoon and also at bedtime. This means that they are nice and clean for school.'

'We pack up with all the animals (dogs, baboons, apes, cats, goat-lings) for a long trek over the veld.'

Holidays with families and friends were always full of excitement:

'The bloody train got off at last,
The expedition's off together,
Destination Bushman's River...
First of all comes 'Suds' that's me,
In charge of this damn safari
And when the holiday is o'er,
You're much more buggered than before...' and so on for
    18 ripe stanzas.

'The breakers (at Amanzimtoti) are huge and you would laugh to see Al and Jimmy caught by the waves and chucked yards up the beach.'

After his dramatic rescue of a swimmer in the shark-infested waters:

'I made a beeline for the pub and had a bottle of whisky ordered on the poor bastard's account.'

On a very choppy, deep-sea fishing trip:

'Mill was clean out and didn't give a damn whether the ship was shelled or torpedoed... I haven't laughed so long in a long time.'

And there was always some melodrama at home at the lake to terrify our poor mother:

'One day the damn (wild) bees went mad. The wife tried to save one of her pet hens but she was so badly stung that we had to do a rescue stunt and eventually had to rush her to a doctor for treatment.'

'One other treatment we have here is snakes. The biggest I shot last season was a beauty – over five feet long.'

'During Christmas and New Year we had an average of 11 drowning accidents per day, but fortunately we managed to yank them all out without any fatal results.'

Schooling was a bit of an afterthought, but my academic successes were proudly acknowledged as I was a dunce at swimming:

'Al is considered quite brilliant.'

And when the time came for us to leave:

'Hell of a day here; getting everything ready for the kids leaving. Mill is quite frantic over the whole business. We've done our best for them and what faults you find must be blamed on their uncle. Anyway I don't think you will be disappointed with them.'

Sadly, our very reluctant return to our war-weary parents brought great and lasting family unhappiness. We were both by then boisterous, outspoken, colonial teenagers bustling with health and energy, and compete misfits at home and at school. Years later when my cousin Jimmy visited Cardiff, our poor mother told him:

'I lost my children to South Africa.'

When in turn my brother Doug revisited South Africa, Auntie Milly greeted him with:

'Here's my other son, back again at last.'

On busy days at the lake, Uncle Jim used to broadcast messages and cheery music to the public over the loudspeakers, always beginning with a hearty:

'Hello, hello, Robinson Lake calling!'

I learned about apartheid and never went back. But still, more than 65 years on, Robinson Lake is still calling me.

A LOVE LETTER AND AN ESCAPE

Margherita Still

FUNNY HOW YOU remember little details when something big happens. I was teaching fractions when I heard about my mum's stroke.

After the funeral as we emptied her house I found a love letter written by Mum on the back of a photograph of her and Dad. It was to reveal a story that had never been told, because the letter wasn't for Dad.

I travelled to my mum's home village in Italy just after her death. It was the first time I had been without her and each day brought more messages of condolence from villagers, making it a difficult holiday.

One evening as I sat outside a café an old man approached and put his hand on my shoulder.

I looked up at him and he put his hand to his chest and announced, 'I am Salvatore.'

I must have look confused but he pulled up a chair and sat down, leaning towards me as he started to tell his story.

This is what I understood of his colloquial Italian as he revealed the story of my mum's life in the village.

Salvatore and my mum Margherita were childhood friends. They fished in the river, searched for wild fruit and generally broke all the rules of their strict Italian families.

They survived World War II and as they reached their teens their friendship strengthened.

As the youngest child my mum was treated like a maid. Her father had a plan to marry her to a rich local gentleman, an older and fatter man than she would choose. She constantly fought her father and refused to be the daughter he expected.

My mum wasn't happy and dreamed of leaving, but money was scarce so it seemed impossible.

Then her elder brother Vito died. This was the only part of the story that I knew. We have a picture of Vito and my mum, a composite made to show them both at the same age, impossible as he died when Mum was young. My mum always told me Vito had been murdered. Vito survived Stalingrad and made his way home, mostly on foot.

He was resourceful to get home and he used this to earn money, smuggling contraband around the local villages. He was saving to marry and promised to take my mum to stay with him and his new bride.

One day he went out on his bike and was killed. My family still argue about his death. My mum and Salvatore both told the same version.

The truck driver said Vito was cycling backwards when he fell in front of the truck. My grandfather hiked up to the snow line to get ice to pack his head wound, but never made it back in time.

Mum never believed it was an accident. When he died only his fiancée and my mum knew where he hid his money, it disappeared.

Then Mum saw the injury that killed him. In southern Italy the ground is so hard that the custom is to reuse graves. After a year they dig up the remains and wrap the bones in muslin before placing them in a wall. As the family were poor they had to do this themselves and my mum had to help. This is when she saw the injury and thought it had been inflicted by an axe and not the road.

The last piece of evidence for Mum was the sudden wealth of the family of the man who knocked Vito over.

My mum's mind was set, she had to leave and Salvatore helped.

For over two years they planned her escape. Salvatore hid a suitcase under his bed that they filled with clothes and money.

After the war, Scotland needed workers and people from all over Europe were invited to take jobs in mills or factories. Salvatore's sister was coming to Scotland and he managed to get the papers she applied with and added my mum's name to the end of the list. No-one knew she was on it.

When they had enough money he went to Salerno for her passport and train tickets, he had to leave the village to buy the tickets because my grandfather was a train driver and the station staff knew Salvatore and my mum. This was to be their biggest challenge, the train guards wouldn't let her board a train.

The night before her escape Salvatore hid her suitcase near the station. In the morning they told their families they were going to pick fruit and headed for the station. They hid in the bushes with the suitcase until the train arrived. Salvatore sneaked the suitcase onto the train and returned to Mum. Only after the train had started to leave did my mum run from her hiding place and jump onto the moving train, being spotted immediately!

It was too late to stop the train, she thought she was free. The station master sent word to her father and he chased her on the next train. He followed to Milan where he gave up because he didn't have papers to cross the border.

Mum travelled on, unaware of how close she came to being stopped. This tiny Italian woman who spoke no English and had never been to a city, travelled alone to Scotland.

The train in Scotland made an unscheduled stop at Stanley where the guard helped her down, then told her to follow the track to the mill that she could see lit up in the distance.

When Salvatore finished his story there was a tear in his eye. He had intended to follow her but could never get away.

I travelled to the village last year and found him again, in the same café he found me in all those years ago. I don't think his own children know the story. Perhaps this family legend belongs to two families, who live thousands of miles apart but are so closely linked by love.

COUSCOUS

Caroline McCarthy

COUSCOUS, TO THINK that the 21st century has seen it become a 'designer' ingredient much loved by celebrity chefs in Britain! John Struthers, I can almost hear your 'Hmph' of disdain at the idea of what you termed 'a mixture of canary seed and sawdust' being so elevated. It was a meagre daily ration of half a cup of 'kush-kush' that was all that kept you and your shipmates from starvation as prisoners of war in Tunisia in the 1940s, a far cry from Granny's Scottish fare. But stay alive you did and came home to tell the tale; but for me, your granddaughter, your death when I was a young girl has meant that I never heard the tale from you in person. Encouraged by my sons I have been piecing together your fascinating story from other sources. The four boys implore me to write down what I know so that it is not forgotten.

Grandad, you have always been an inspiration to me. I recall so many interesting objects in Granny's home, things which you had brought home from faraway places in the course of your career as an Engineer Officer in the Merchant Navy. At one time I actually harboured an ambition to be the first female Chief Engineer – that was until I discovered that Victoria Drummond had beaten me to it, serving with great honour during World War II! Well, I did marry a Merchant Navy Engineer Officer!

My late mother was your daughter and I think she was very like you. From her I learned that you had left the sea to work ashore when she and her sisters were young. However, on the outbreak of World War II, when you were already into your 60s, you volunteered to return to the Merchant Navy, serving on *Empire Defender*, attempting to relieve a siege of Malta. The ship was torpedoed and sank in the Mediterranean, leading to your capture and imprisonment in Tunisia. There was mention of a mutiny, how exciting, but I knew no more until my interest was rekindled following my mother's death.

Among her papers I discovered a cutting from the *Glasgow Herald* of 15 July 1942, referring to seafarers imprisoned in a camp in Tunisia. I thought it must refer to you. So began a voyage of discovery. My son,

Brian, had been a member of a British Schools Exploring Society expedition and in connection with that I received a phone call in 1998 from Admiral Lord Lewin. I knew that he was also the Chairman of the George Cross Island Association and because of this Malta link I chanced my luck and mentioned the story of *Empire Defender*. It caught his interest, too. A very influential man, within days he forwarded information he had obtained from the Maritime Museum at Greenwich.

Mutiny there was, indeed, Grandad! While preparing for the ship's departure from Glasgow, the 'sarang' (bosun) of the lascar crew had a recurring dream that the ship would be 'calash' (finished – sunk) before the next new moon! Absolutely nothing, neither incentives nor threats, would induce these men to sail. They left the vessel and camped on the quay! Eventually, white ratings had to be employed, at considerable expense, and the vessel sailed, disguised and changing its name when passing through French and Spanish waters.

So near and yet so far! You almost reached Malta with your cargo of desperately needed armaments but an enemy aircraft saw you and launched a torpedo, with devastating results – in accordance with the sarang's dream! How did we find out the next bit? Does it surprise you, Grandad, that your adventurous spirit has continued through the generations and took young Brian to work in Iraq? One evening out there he idly searched online for *Empire Defender*. Back here, my husband was checking his emails when I heard a shout. He had received an excited message from Brian. On the internet, Brian had found a 'survivor's report' from a member of the crew, the Second Engineer, a Mr J.S. Struthers! Grandad, it was like hearing you tell your story to us in person! The details of your capture, support, overt and covert, from the Maltese community in Tunisia, the conditions in which you were held (including the starvation rations I have spoken of), the life-saving contribution of the Red Cross; all were there. And we learned how you were eventually released and, with the help of the ironically named American Consul, Mr Doolittle, repatriated to Scotland. There was no advance notice of your arrival. I believe Granny answered a knock at the door one day and there you were, gaunt but alive!

A visit to the National Archives at Kew yielded a wealth of original documents; hand-written crew lists, correspondence about your imprisonment and even the identity label you would have carried on your release! Many years later, and in another century from you, Grandad, I am sailing through the same Mediterranean waters as you did. I am on board a container ship and my husband is the Chief Engineer. I would love to know what you make of that! We may even be over the wreck of *Empire Defender*. I think of you. The torpedo hit its mark. You waited for orders. None came so you went to collect your life jacket. You went back to turn off the steam to stop the engines, went on deck and slid down a rope into the lifeboat. The ship sank. You could only await your fate.

As we approach Malta, I watch from the bridge as we move slowly into harbour. There is just time for Bill and me to have a quick tour of the island. We see the enormous bell, the monument to those who served in the Malta Convoys and we think how fortunate we are. Grandad, your story lives on. Soon my little granddaughter will come to know it, and why our family exchange knowing smiles at the mention of couscous!

GRAND UNCLE JAMES

John Flett

GRAND UNCLE JAMES was a tramp, a hobo. His father was a small but successful shopkeeper and his siblings were engaged in the business or in other respectable pursuits in Orkney, but James was a rover. He had no exciting vices such as drink, women, or gambling, simply an inability to stay in one place or stick to one job for longer than nine to 12 months. The result was that about 30 years after leaving school he had been in most areas of the world – crewman on a tramp-steamer trading in the China Sea and Indian Ocean, working in a diamond mine in South Africa, not to mention a year rounding up cattle on an Argentinean hacienda. The following incident happened in New South Wales, Australia.

James had just completed a spell of work on a big sheep station and accordingly had to move on. By good luck he heard of a similar job on a neighbouring station, 'neighbouring' meaning, in Australian sheep country, about 30 miles distant. Knowing the area, he decided to walk over, carrying his tiny one-man tent and sleeping bag, and some simple rations. He reckoned that he could cover the distance, walking in the cooler parts of the day, in two days.

As darkness fell on the first day of his journey, he pitched his wee tent, brewed up some tea and had his supper. James was about to go to bed when he heard moaning and a vocal gasping. Alarmed, but certain it was no wild animal he went in the direction of the sound and discovered a man staggering and falling on to his knees, obviously exhausted and parched with thirst. James took him in hand back to the tent, gave him some fluid and put him onto the sleeping bag where he fell immediately to sleep.

In the morning, after some solid food and more liquid the stranger became quite talkative and after a bit said to Uncle James, 'You're no Aussie, I guess that by your accent you're Scotch.' Like a good Orcadian James admitted that this was true, but only partly. 'I come from a place called Orkney which you've never heard of but which is actually off the north coast of Scotland.' The stranger replied, 'I know where Orkney is and I've been there.'

He went on. 'It was like this. When I was about seven or eight years old my folks took me with them on a holiday to Orkney and

Shetland, and in Orkney we lived in a boarding-house near the harbour. Don't remember much about the holiday except for one experience I do recall, maybe because I got hurt. With some of the local lads I went out along the shore not far from the pier till we came to some grassy banks which got steeper and steeper till they were almost cliffs. These boys scrambled up like monkeys, and I, keen to show I was just as tough, climbed after them. Inevitably I lost all footholds and handholds, rolled down to land on the stony beach where I lay roaring my head off with pain and humiliation. One of the local boys descended with more skill and dignity than I had done, picked me up, and declared that his mum would fix up my several cuts, scratches and bruises.'

The stranger was now into his stride and went on, 'When we got to his home his mum was baking. She wiped her floury hands on her apron, bathed all my sore bits, and applied iodine: boy! Did it sting! Then she took one of her pancakes, still warm, spread it with syrup and gave it to me: the finest food I've ever tasted.'

'Funny that,' said Uncle James. 'The baking lady was my mum and I was the youngster who took you home.'

THE BANDITS AND THE BRIDE

Sara Grady

MY GREAT, GREAT grandfather was a true blue, Wild West cowboy
He and his brothers were a rabble. A wild bunch. A posse. The sort
of horse-riding fiends you'd warn your daughters about.

They robbed a bank once (I like to think like an early John
Dillinger) and were chased all the way to Mexico. On the lam. What
a great phrase, and apt: antiquated but still sharp around the edges.

After laying low a while I suppose they must have seen the error
of their ways or perhaps got bored. Either way they crept back
over the border unscathed a few years later.

In the Oklahoma Land Rush the government sold off plots of
land 'bought' from the natives at a dollar an acre, and these enter-
prising gentlemen bought a plot. One hopes to settle into a decent
farm life like the rest of the prairie folk.

Well, it wasn't too long before the feminine touch was going
wanting about the place. So the oldest brother (my great-great-grand-
father which is far too grand a title for a bandit like him) decided
to get himself a wife. Maybe the townsfolk remembered Mexico.
Or maybe he just didn't like the look of the local girls. One or the
other he found (and brought home) Celene.

She was a French opera singer with a stunning voice I'm told.
Whether she was a mail-order bride looking for a fresh start or she
was dragged from a New Orleans saloon stage I know not. In any
case, she arrived on the farm. And there they all lived, the gang of
reformed outlaws and their formerly glamorous French wife.

As a child, I saw it in the candyfloss pastels of a Rodgers &
Hammerstein musical. A real life *Seven Brides for Seven Brothers*
In my teenage imaginings it was a rather more sordid affair: seven
burly bandits and one (fallen-on-hard-times) chanteuse. There were
often fishnets and whisky and tinkling sad pianos involved, but then
what would you expect from a wildly romantic and depressive teen?

I always imagine her arriving at the modest house in that jewel-
toned silk trimmed with black Chantilly lace so favoured by the
ladies in Westerns. A net-veiled hat perched on paper-rolled ringlets.
Lace gloves, perhaps a bustle. Respectable. Beautiful. A complete fish
out of water.

I hope Celene was glamorous and wild – for what would possess someone to take a rugged criminal up on an offer like that? Why did she go? Where did she come from? Was her life before an amazing Parisian dream? I doubt it, if she agreed to this fate.

Was she disappointed with the handmade dilapidated clapboard house they'd built her? Relieved at the smallness of this anonymous life out in the horizon? I'll never know now. Her daughter never knew her (the replacement wife saw fit that she was shipped to an orphanage sharpish after Celene's tragically early death), and even she's passed away now.

When I was young and doing a 'family history' homework assignment, my grandmother showed me an old photo of the brothers outside the house they had built. It was the first time I heard this story, but by no means the last time it'd be told. (I regaled my in-laws with it the first time we met. I thought they ought to know what sort of family they were getting involved with.) But I've never seen a photo of Celene. I'm not sure any have survived. The new wife probably got rid of those too.

Though even without many records (can you expect a clean papertrail in circumstances like this?) her legend lives on. An exotic and talented woman once went looking for adventure in the wilds of America. And she probably ended up with far more than she bargained for.

I've often hoped I inherited her sense of adventure, I know I'm one of few in the clan who carry her operatic inclinations. And I hoped desperately in my youth to capture her allure – even if I've made it up a bit in all my retellings, papering over the dusty cracks of this old tale with my own imagination. That's the beauty of legends I suppose. They keep on growing, long after the dust has settled on the prairie.

LEGEND OF THE DROWNING CHILDREN – LEGEND OF COUNTRY

Farhan

THIS LEGEND GOES back to the time of my mum's childhood as it is set in her homeland Bangladesh. Bangladesh is a developing country of which I know very little as I was born here in Scotland. I have visited twice and it has given me a glimpse of how hard life is there

Many homes in Bangladesh are very simply structured and often do not have the luxuries we have like a big bath. Many families have to take their bath/shower in a pool situated in front of the village and it is shared by all the villagers. The pool is fairly deep so it is vital that everyone knows how to swim.

This legend tells the story of young boy named Ali who at the age of four was very inquisitive and was always looking for adventure One day Ali walked all the way to the pool where at midday it was deserted. Ali thought he could see a beautiful swan swimming in the pool, he was awestruck by this beautiful mirage and as he gazed at it, it called Ali so Ali walked towards the swan to the middle of the pool and was never seen again.

Ali's mum Aisha finished her household chores and discovered Ali was not in the house and she ran frantically and called all the villagers out to help search for her son. At sunset the villagers found the body floating in the pool and as they pulled the body out they knew it was Ali. They could see the imprint of a hand on Ali's body The village spiritualist came to the scene and told everyone the bad spirits had pushed Ali into the pool hence the imprint of the hand

Ali's mum was too devastated to come and see the body of her drowned son. For many days and many nights, Aisha would continue to search for her son and one night she thought she could see Ali calling her from the pool with his arms stretched out. Aisha walked toward him and she too drowned. The villagers never found her body but since then, there has never been a drowning of a child in that pool. The villagers believe Aisha is protecting the pool.

MY FAMILY LEGEND

Bethany Carlin

IN 1988 MY AUNT MARY, who is a nurse, lived and worked in a town called Loroguma in Kenya. She was there for two years with a group of nurses who worked voluntarily. My aunty had to deal with upsetting moments but managed to help families in need of care. This is a story that was a memory from her time there that she will never forget.

A mother and her five-year-old son from the Turkana tribe had arrived at the clinic in the early afternoon after having walked many miles. Her son was very ill with malaria and needed treatment urgently. It was decided to take him to the nearest hospital for treatment and a blood transfusion. Unfortunately this was during the rainy season so main roads were flooded and unable to be driven on. The only other option was to give him a blood transfusion at the clinic. Although his mother or father would have been the best donor, his mother was expecting a baby and his father was many miles away working. So they tested the boy's blood type in the lab and it came back A-positive. My Aunt Mary was also A-positive so she volunteered to give him her blood and a chance of survival. After the transfusion he gradually got better and in a few days he had fully recovered. The boy's mum was so grateful that she called my aunty the boy's second mother.

MOCCASIN BILL

Laura Morrison-Smith

(A re-imagining of a half-remembered tale)

THE WHOLE VILLAGE has come to see him off, the way Vikings used to send their dead kings to sea in burning ships, the women weeping and the men stern and solemn. He turns for the last time at the bend of the road that forks into dirt tracks leading east and west. As he waves he can see his wife and tiny daughter standing apart from the others, just beyond the heat of the bonfire. Their shadows are giants behind them, Bible-black and dancing.

Bill had come to Saskatchewan in the autumn of 1909, working his way from town to town, relying on his easy wit and bar-room bravura to land himself seasonal work and beds for the night. He had tried painting portraits in the busier towns – 10 cents a pencil sketch, 15 a watercolour – but found the intimacy of it uncomfortable, following the curve of a cheekbone, plunging into the glittering flecks of an iris. He missed the open spaces anyway, the sweep of the moorland and the cut-glass dome of the sky. The village he had settled in was nestled deeply in the dark forests between the highest mountains in the state. And there was a girl, a princess of the Cree, and the land was lush and fertile, and he had to settle somewhere.

* * *

Bill had been walking all day, the snow deepening the higher he climbed. It was nine weeks since the last tradesman had made it through this pass and the village's supplies were almost spent. Three of the old women had gone, the cold easily penetrating their papery skin. But two days ago they had buried the first child, a 14-month-old boy who quietly froze between his parents one bitter night. Bill had volunteered to go for help the night before, standing before the community elders in the Big House, quietly resolute despite their protestations. He had married the daughter of the chief, Jemima, dark and wild, who danced in the thunderstorm on his first night in the village and kissed him slyly behind the missionary's cabin as the old man taught carols to the children. In truth, the journey was suicide and the men would not allow their own sons to go. The snow had fallen relentlessly all winter and the steep passage to the nearest town would be packed with unnavigable ice.

As he climbs, a fat, butter moon throbs through the hatched cloud, throwing the rocks into gigantic shadows stooping over the narrow path, dwarfing the solitary climber. His progress is slow as he negotiates the slippery ascent, his moccasins tied to the wide-framed snowshoes. Muttering a Gaelic psalm under his breath, he repeats it like an incantation, the words elongated and melodic. He imagines the craggy pass a hall of winds resounding with the music of his homeland, swelling and rolling like the sound of the sea. He is not a nostalgic man, but here, in this great, echoing cathedral of ice, he sees his memories before him, crowds of ghosts gathering in the failing light.

* * *

Bill is a glutton for beauty, sustaining himself on the fragile grace of the skeletal moon, the flayed black nerves of winter trees. It is always night here, even at her height the sun is widowed in sooty veils. The snow is falling lightly as he walks on, over the icy switchback ridges that serve as paths. It has been six days and he should have reached the other side of the pass and been on his way back from the town with help and supplies. The cold is the worst, every part of his skin that isn't covered with furs and sealskins burns white-hot, but the hunger is getting to him now, a dull foetal ache swallowing him up from the inside.

The morning he left his birthland had been no different to any other day. He rises early, lights the stove and makes the porridge, stirring it carefully, watching the skin forming on the back of the spoon. Walking to the gate to fetch the milk he suddenly sees the road, as if for the first time, winding on and on under his feet, leaping over streams, stretching past fields and houses and tapering into the horizon. He doesn't stop walking till he reaches the sea, the grinning crescent of the pier, the waiting ship and the sharp points of light in the darkening distance he mistakes for the lamps of America.

On the mountain he remembers his father teaching him the alphabet on the beach, carving tall, spindly letters into the wet sand

and then, later in the day, as his mother rubbed the sand from his feet with a rough rag, he watched the mysterious symbols wash away, the waves rolling interminably, the swiftly turning pages of a book without end.

* * *

Bill eats his moccasins on the seventh day, chewing purposefully as he walks, barefoot, whistling a tune, his footprints deep shadows in the powdery drifts. The first quills of smoke rise from the cottages in the awakening town. He will turn the last corner and see it as the sun rises, on top of him before he realises its nearness.

* * *

Forests thicken in the valleys, deep and lovely, stretching to the starry heights. The lakes teem with movement, quickening with all kinds of life. In the towns the houses have crept up the side of the mountain now and the roads are wide and smooth with gas stations, telephones and signs that point out tricky bends and precipitous inclines.

The snow still falls in dreamy waltzes, falling on the dark pines, falling on William Mackenzie's headstone, worn smooth by the seasons, falling on the ruins of the old villages, falling in sweeping waves, deep and dazzling in the sunlight.

Local Legends

THE GIZZEN BRIGGS

C.F. Ross

'MAN THE OARS!' The Skipper shrieked above the gale which bomb-arded the Dornoch Firth in 1963. They were a few miles from the infamous Gizzen Briggs which was hidden in the squall.

The crew of the 30-foot coble working the mussel scalps was battered about as the two engines failed and white spumes flooded the deck. A westerly wind was going against an incoming tide to adverse effect. Three to an oar and two bailing out water was useless, and as a last resort the Skipper shouted:

'Jettison the mussels, lads, before we end up in Norway!'

The crew and the Skipper were hard-pushed to lose their cargo and wages but they were floundering in the firth, and in the battle one long oar suddenly split. Mr Allan M. Ross, in his teens like the other oarsmen, tumbled onto the deck. He tried to regain his footing and grabbed a smaller oar which still didn't help them steer into shore. There were no life jackets aboard and every one now was reconciled to their fate – Davy Jones' Locker.

However there was sudden mercy from the sea gods Poseidon and Neptune which brought an unexpected lull in the gale. The crew's efforts emptying their catch and consequently lightening their sinking vessel, allowed them to manoeuvre into shore near Ardjachie Point.

In 1921 Adam Holm Ross was born in Tain, Ross and Cromarty Scotland, and was the youngest of eight children. He was named Holm, after a distant relative on his grandmother's side who was a lengendary fisherman.

Adam grew up to be a beloved uncle of the Ross clan in Tain, and before his army unit was posted to North Africa in 1939, the young blade kept people rapt with his stories and wit.

However, in the early '50s after the war, he was a bachelor and lived alone. He had become more reclusive but sometimes walked Tain Hill with his young nephew Allan. The weather was such one day as they looked to sea, there before them lay the wrecked Gizzen Briggs, and they heard strange murmurs coming from the firth. Allan loved to hear tales of olden times and family legends and that day Adam told this story:

'A group of workmen were out on the Gizzen Briggs completing their mammoth task of building a four mile bridge between Dornoch Point and Morrich More on the sand banks. This was most dangerous because few people knew the safe route between the sinking sand beds. Legend had it a local fishseller, his horse and fully-loaded cart had vanished there one stormy night.

'The construction was going fairly well until the spring tides turned and with the higher waves and winds, the Gizzen Briggs was scuppered. It was tragic that so much labour had come to nothing, and even worse, men were marooned on the banks.

'It was at this anxious moment a fisherman called Adam Holm decided he must save them. He told no-one because he'd be called a lunatic and he would probably be stopped. He was a quiet loner named after the area where he lived, and in Ross-shire Holm meant 'raised islet'. He soon set sail on this perilous trip from which they may not return.

'Nonetheless Adam found the stranded workers and after a soaking trip back to land, he took them to his hut on the raised dunes of Morrich More. They dried themselves near his fire, were fed and Adam gave them a tot of whisky to help them recover from their watery ordeal.

'The workmen knew Adam Holm had done this good deed selflessly and for no reward. He hadn't cared who they were or where they came from. It was then they divulged to him that in fact they weren't humans at all but "faeries". He was the only person to know about their existence in the Firth which was solely to rebuild the Gizzen Briggs.

'No matter how many times it collapsed, they would return as soon as the weather permitted to start construction again.

'Adam Holm was a level-headed chap who found it hard to believe he'd saved "faeries". Then a few days after they'd recovered one asked him:

'Faeries have a great problem with the open sea and cannot cross wild water without help. Please will you kindly take us back whilst there is calm? We will be eternally grateful and will of course repay you in kind. Our gift to you is that from now on, every generation of fishermen with the name Holm, or relatives of the afore-mentioned, will never drown at sea. You must, however, agree that all we have discussed is kept secret.'

'Adam Holm was not a man to believe in faery prophecies but if true, it would be an amazing gift for seafaring folk like him, his sons and their sons, and their kith and kin. He wasn't a talkative man anyway, and keeping a secret would be easy for him. After they'd gone, and he was once again alone in his hut fixing his nets, he felt an assured calm within and a happy allegiance with Neptune.'

By late 1963, as a result of experiences in World War II, Adam Holm Ross lived a quiet, almost isolated life in Tain. But one of his nephews, Mr Allan M. Ross, a 17-year-old, often called to get Adam to tell his stories again. But the latter could not be drawn into any discussion about what happened in the firth.

However Allan suspected the Holm legend had something to do with saving him and the rest of the crew of their stricken coble off Ardjachie Point. But as a teenager Allan would never, ever admit to anyone, even his uncle, that he believed in faeries.

DUNDEE'S FIRST FLOODLIT BOXING MATCH

Mark McGowan

THIS STORY COMES from my Uncle Ben, Dundee's famous window cleaner, no any actual blood relation but that is the way it is around here. The times I've listened to your ranting and complaining, but now you're gone and just your stories remain, I would give plenty to hear them again. Hope everyone enjoys this story I have endured a dozen times and only now understand the value of. Wee Benny, miss you pal.

It was a night not fit for a washing line to be out! The rain had just stopped but the chimney reek and constant drizzle meant you could see everything you were breathing. That oasis of shelter in the dark, grey air, with a fire in the grate shining out like only that old place could. A working man's pub in a working man's city. Set on the straight stretch of Lochee High Street, when Lochee High Street was Lochee High Street. I remember the place was always thick with tobacco smoke that seemed thicker than the wee half-curtains set at the windows. Clean mind you, Big Benny G. who had the place always kept it clean, had a team of Lochee wives go through the place every morning. Two doors and all the windows open, brush pole across the door meant you were no getting served any earlier; actually no-one got to set foot in the place till the floor had dried. Those wee Lochee wives had a look all their own, half-hunched backs, head squares, swollen knuckles on red hands and powerful forearms like hams from Mr Falconer's butcher's shop window. Always two pairs of shoes, one for working in, one for going home in '... Cause you never know who you might meet sonny.'

It must have been a Thursday night. I was home on leave from the army, no conscription for me. I joined the regulars – the extra bob a week, better treatment and if you ran away your time still counted – all might have had something to do with that. Close to the tattie holidays so October month. So none but the bravest souls had come out for a pint and a nip. At the time Benny G. had a lassie working behind the bar till his wife put a stop to that.

How this got started is a mystery to this day but Ronnie

Gallagher's son, young Billy from the Eagle Mills, was insisting that the miley, the dismantled railway track, started at the Marchbanks and ran south towards Harefield Road. Matty McKay the docker was not having this, the old railway line ran up northwards, his face and neck were already red from the drink when I got there and I knew it was best to agree with or leave him well alone when he got like that. Before anyone knew what was happening they had decided between themselves that they were going to have it out in a proper, out-in-the-street fashion.

Well big Benny was having none of this and threw them each out the separate doors, Matty McKay he lifted off the floor and tipped out into the street. There a plan was hatched to meet up at the Camperdown Park. At this time there were no more than five taxis on the roads so Ratty Finlayson took Matty home with him and got his father's coal truck. Young Billy, punching the air along the way with a few kicks thrown in for good measure, walked with the rest of us in a big crowd up to the park. The further we walked the bigger the talk got of how he was going to knock him out, a left there, he punched the air, a might right there, a short amateurish upper cut. We were there in no time and as word had got round that a fight was in the offing the crowd seemed to have grown, some women and older children had joined the crowd. It took me to stay standing up and keep hands off young Billy that were intent on slapping his back like he had already won the fight.

I think everyone was as surprised as me to see the coal truck there, not only as lorries in them days had a top speed of 25 miles per hour but for Mr Finlayson to allow Ratty to take the coal truck out after nine o'clock. Two cars had now joined us and seemed to set the outdoor arena alight with their lamps. They were the most sober things there as the crowd dared not push up against the vehicles but happily pushed each other. I had not noticed how the rain had started lashing down again until I saw it falling in the yellow beams. The noise of the crowd near knocked my hat off as Matty got out of the cab in his vest and put a coal sack on the wheel arch of the truck. Billy looked like he was trying to take off, he was flapping his arms up and down so fast, shouting something while sticking his chin out. His first punch was a straight right high over Matty's left shoulder which took them to the floor. Now in some sort of sinew-popping embrace, each with one arm trapped under them, it looked like they would be shouting at each other all night. Then a fevered punch-for-punch exchange to the body was broken when young Billy started trying to bring his boots into it. About three men lurched forward, I would say they were no more than light slaps on their legs but that knocked all the strength out of the two wrestlers. By now women had rushed in and started to slap at the would-be referee men, pulling and slapping them to far greater effect. I was not too much caring about who was hitting who or how they did it – I did want a clear view of it but there was not much else to see. Two men, steam rising off them like prize horses, hugging like long lost brothers, whispering in each other's ears.

So there, as quick as it had started, it was over and we had a long, cold walk home. Home was the only place left to go as the pubs shut at ten o'clock in them days and that I can tell you was Dundee's first floodlit boxing match.

THE SHIP IN THE CHURCH

Gail Squires

THE STORY OF William Dunlop, my great, great, great grandfather is amazing and legendary within our family. I think it better if he tells his own story...

'In 1797 at Cape St Vincent, Spain and Britain were engaged in a battle of ferocious proportions. Standing guard on the deck of the defeated *San Josef*, I was quite alone, isolated by a thick pall of smoke from cannons blasting continuously on all sides. As I listened to the raging battle, my thoughts wandered to the last time I had seen my homeland on a sharply cold, blustery night in November.

'I had been walking home along the seafront, my body bent into the wind buffeting against me, when out of the darkness I was set upon by invisible assailants and bundled away onto a ship before I could resist. By the time I was allowed on deck, there had been nothing but ocean around me, Scotland had gone, I was a Gunner's Mate and I was heading to war.

'Back on the *San Josef*, these thoughts were interrupted by another sailor who approached me in an odd, diffident manner. An alarm bell rang somewhere in the back of my mind that was still partly in Scotland, and as he got closer I saw that he was not only a stranger but was wearing an unfamiliar uniform. My solitary few moments of daydreaming had cost me the sharpness of mind that would have alerted me a few pivotal seconds earlier. It was by then too late and I found myself captured once more, this time by the Spanish navy.

'Many days and weeks passed and, as a prisoner of war, I had been as good as left to rot with about 20 others in the same cell. As the weeks lengthened into months, many died around me, many of them from simple despair. I remember clearly sitting on a cold stony floor in that dismal dungeon surrounded by pitiful souls, all praying for deliverance, but not with any hope or expectation. I hoped that as He looked down on us He would see, amidst all the gloom and misery, a pale but persistent glow of faith emanating from his servant, William Dunlop. If He looked closer and read my heart, He would have found no despair in there, no lack of expectation, nothing but hope and belief. I didn't believe myself to be more worthy of being rescued than anyone else, I didn't even expect to be rescued. What I did expect and believe was that God would make the decisions about my fate and that would be the fate I deserved.

'Unoccupied time hung heavy on my hands and I began to fear that my mind would deteriorate as some of those around me had. I had come to feel a responsibility for helping my companions as well as myself to evade that ruinous melancholy and malaise that had afflicted so many others and so I set myself the task of finding some way of occupying our time and thereby diverting our thoughts in more healthy directions. I found myself thinking about the ships I had served on and one frigate in particular was often on my mind. I found that with concentration I could remember it in startling detail, its 50 guns, rigging, and decks. So, I decided to try making a model of it and started the process of finding materials to do so. I told a cellmate of my plan and asked if he would help me so word soon got around and we all had the project in common. Even the guards would sometimes hand me in bits and pieces that I could use, including shards of glass and sharp metal that would take the place of traditional tools. With the collaboration of my companions, this flotsam and jetsam began to take shape as the pieces that I hoped would eventually come together as the frigate. I began to think of her as the *Caledonia* and so she became inextricably linked with my conviction that I would return to Scotland and my family one day. Bit by bit, it came together and one day was completed. Our pleasure was great, nobody had fallen into despair while we were absorbed in the ship and it became famous throughout the prison. Nobody damaged or belittled it and that was more amazing than anything else in a place like that.

'Late one night I was awakened by the clear light of the moon from a cloudless sky. It had edged its way through the bars on the windows high above me and was staring, exultantly, into my face – I knew that the time we would be freed was soon. The very next day, with the help of my cellmates, I began to dismantle the ship and carefully placed the parts in a kit bag handed in by one of the guards. I promised that I would, if I got home, reconstruct it and present it to the church in my home town in thanks for our deliverance of which I was certain. I eventually arrived back in Saltcoats on a warm spring evening with hope, gratitude and wonderment in my heart and the constituent parts of the *Caledonia* safely in my kit bag.

'The rest of my life story unfolds in an unspectacular fashion. My certainty that my liberation was thanks to God spurred me on with renewed purpose. I kept my word and at last, in 1804, I was honoured to wheel the reconstructed *Caledonia* ceremoniously in a barrow to the church through the streets of Saltcoats with the people of the town cheering me on. The ship was suspended on chains high above the congregation and for the rest of my lifetime it remained there, appearing to sail ethereally on a sea of faith in God.'

The ship can be seen to this day in St Cuthbert's Church, Saltcoats.

BENEDICTO'S BATTLE

Lucy Crolla

IT STARTED OFF just a normal working day for my great grandad, Benedicto. Little did he know he was about to get into a bit of trouble. This is how it all started...

Germany was at war with Britain. Italy decided they were on Germany's side but that was a bit of a problem for Benedicto. He was Italian but had travelled to Scotland many years ago to settle with his family. He had settled down in a little fishing village called Newhaven and had opened an ice cream shop.

Benedicto was quite a serious man but was very kind and thoughtful towards his customers. At Christmas he would give all his customers a packet of biscuits each as a present.

On that day Benedicto was working hard in his shop when suddenly he heard a loud BANG!!! My great grandad rushed to the window to see what the noise was. He couldn't believe his eyes when he saw a huge gang of people coming along the street waving sticks and throwing stones. They were a Leith gang and they had been attacking all the Italian shops because Italy was against Scotland in the war. Benedicto was terrified because he knew they were coming for him!

Suddenly, out of the corner of his eye he saw lots of fishwives running down the street towards the shop. They all joined together to form a huge barrier in front of the shop. They had all heard the gang and had come to help him.

The Leith gang came face to face with the Newhaven fishwives. There was no way the fishwives were going to let the gang anywhere near Benedicto or the shop! The battle began, stones were thrown, windows were broken but the fishwives were not moving. Soon the Leith gang realised they were not going to win this battle and they all started to go home.

The fishwives started to cheer but no-one was cheering as loudly as Benedicto! The fishwives had saved him because he was loved so much by all the locals and he was so happy.

Benedicto ran his ice cream shop for many years after that and his business was passed on to his son, Tony and then to his grandson Mark, who is my dad.

THE DUCKS

Iona Staniforth

MY FAMILY LEGEND is a story I have been told by my grandpa. During the war my grandpa was very little (one to seven years old) and he couldn't remember very much about it but his father (my great grandfather) had told him many stories about it, which my grandpa has passed on to me.

The story begins when my grandpa would have been about two years old. He lived in Buckie (a small village in the North East of Scotland). Towards the edge of the village there was an old whisky distillery, where whisky was made and stored. One day a German bombing plane passing by dropped a bomb by accident, probably meant for Glasgow. The bomb soared through the air, smashing into the whisky distillery at full speed, sending whisky exploding out in all directions. Luckily, because the bomb hit towards the edge of the village no-one was killed or badly injured.

Once the village had been given the all clear and people were safe to come out of their shelters, some villagers went out to investigate what damage had been done. The only damage they found was to the whisky distillery, which was now a complete wreck. As the villagers stood staring at the remains, one man shouted out and pointed down the small hill towards a pond.

'The ducks! Look at the ducks!' he shouted.

They all ran down to the edge of the pond where they saw the ducks staggering and toppling around the place. It took them a while to notice the stream of whisky running down into the pond which the ducks were eagerly drinking from.

And that is my family legend. Not about a famous war hero or about an army commander, no, it's about a bomb that caused ducks to get drunk.

JAMES HOPKINS AND THE HIGHWAYMAN

Rosemary Richey

THE LEGEND WAS passed on to me when I visited the old farmhouse at Stradreagh where my maternal grandfather grew up. I remember driving along the undulating mountain road with my mother, my uncle and my two sisters to the spot where the Murderhole turns off to Bolea to see where the unnamed ancestor killed the highwayman. There must have been a sense of anticipation. I do not think it necessarily was met. When we arrived the spot was unremarkable. The long straw-coloured grass swayed in the breeze. The warmth of the sun turned cold where the cool mountain air juxtaposed itself onto my face. I can feel the stillness, hear the faint rustle of forest trees in the near distance and twitch at the memory of the moist sucking movement of the boggy earth beneath my feet.

I revisited the townland in October of last year with my children. Returning from our daily excursions, with no houses along the road to light the way, the blackness enveloped me, making me doubt where I was. I could put my foot on the accelerator and sail up the steep inclines (seven hills from the start of the road to my aunt's holiday cottage at Stradreagh) but 200 years ago, with a horse and cart and no protection from the elements, only the brave would have journeyed this route at night.

On the sunny afternoon of my childhood, my mother told the story in unelaborated form. An ancestor travelling home along the road to Stradreagh was attacked by a highwayman. He killed the highwayman, turned himself in to the authorities, but was exonerated because he was acting in self defence. I did not question the lack of detail or the black and white morality of the evil highwayman and my heroic ancestor in this homily to the fortitudes of the Covenanting farmers of 18th century County Londonderry. I accepted and adopted it as a metaphor for a family narrative of civic and spiritual virtue spanning the generations, one to the next.

Once the initial burst of enthusiasm that followed my decision to take part in the Scottish Book Trust project subsided, I realised that, while I believed I knew the full details surrounding the end of the unlamented highwayman, in fact I knew little. The farmhouse was demolished in 1991, my mother and uncle both died within weeks of each other six years ago. In the internet age I hoped others might help. A keyword search revealed that there were several highwaymen patrolling the Murderhole Road in the late 18th and early 19th centuries – not just the one killed by my ancestor. 'My' highwayman was Cushy Glen. I found a local history website devoted to Limavady and made contact with the webmaster's wife. It transpired that it was not a McIlmoyle (my grandfather's surname) who killed Cushy but a Hopkins. I contacted an aunt who posted over my grandmother's family tree. Her mother, my great grandmother, had been a Hopkins and it is through her that I have proof of being related to James Hopkins, my great, great, great, great, great uncle.

Mrs Lueg went on to tell me a more morally muted tale than the one my mother had incanted. In 1799, angered by almost 20 years of infringements on their lives and property, the farmers and tradesmen of Stradreagh and Bolea decided to entrap the recalcitrant highwayman. James Hopkins was selected to lead the assault. The family tree notes that only the year before Cushy's death another Hopkins brother, John, had taken part in the 1798 United Irish Rebellion and had had to emigrate to America to evade arrest. If a brother could fight King and country to improve the lot of his fellow Irishmen, killing a highwayman would have been a paltry act in comparison. At the hotel in Bridge Street, Coleraine where Glen loitered looking for potential victims, James Hopkins and his friends flashed money and watches, knowing Cushy would take the bait. They enticed Cushy into following James home and then, when Cushy made his move, James killed him, claiming to have acted in self defence.

The Northern Constitution of 5 April 1978 quotes, 'It is said that after shooting Cushy, James lifted the body, placed it in the cart and took it along to the Glen Cabin where Mrs Glen, who aided and abetted her husband, waited. 'Did you get the money all right Paddy?' she called out in the dark. 'No, he got no money but something he's been seeking for a long time,' replied James Hopkins. Hopkins was a man of cold justice, who no doubt felt vindicated by the 20 shallow graves that were later found dotted among the bogside of the Murderhole Road.

I like to think I have discovered a new family narrative. The core of virtue and social responsibility is still there and in many ways

James Hopkins is more heroic. He knowingly placed himself in danger. Hopkins may have been a paladin, but a shard of ruthlessness had pierced his conscience. My family like to tell a tale of victimhood turning to heroism and a resolute adherence to the law even to your own personal cost, but Hopkins choose to take another man's life and to pass it off as self defence. This courageous act of manumission safeguarded Hopkin's well-being and the well-being of his neighbours but flew in the face of God and the law. When retold my new legend to an aunt and cousin there was a momentary silence; then, 'No, we have never heard *that* story,' they said and the conversation moved on.

Great Grandparents

CRAIG'S ROAD

Iain Brown

IN THE HIGHLANDS and islands of Scotland the people have always been famed for their gift, real or alleged, of the 'sight', which is the ability to 'foresee' unpleasant events before they happen.

This is the story about the day my grandfather saved my brother Craig's life. It is unlike any other story I have heard, in that it tells how Grandpa was guided by something unexplainable that day. A premonition which compelled him to act in a way which left him powerless to resist. Like a pawn being guided in a game of chess, he brought Craig back from the other side.

It was the summer of 1978 when my two elder brothers, Craig, aged seven, and Keith, aged nine, had been enjoying their holiday at our grandparents' house in Brae, Shetland. They had taken particular interest in recreating their favourite moments of the 1978 World Cup finals, when Ally's army had beaten Holland in style but failed to qualify for the second stages.

The oil industry was booming in the north of Scotland following the discovery of the Ninian and Brent oil fields. Sullom Voe oil terminal was still under construction and with up to 6,000 people being employed, it was one of the biggest construction sites in Europe.

Our grandfather, Captain Christopher James Nicolson, was the deputy harbour master at Sullom Voe, a position which required great responsibility and knowledge, qualities which he had in abundance following many years as a master mariner.

He was a man of large stature with a kind and gentle nature and was raised on a croft in Weisdale, Shetland, in an era when academic ability was key to a better life.

His moral values seem to have been passed down through the generations and are testament to the teachings of his forebear John Nicolson, who introduced the Methodist faith to Shetland in 1819.

The morning of the incident had begun like any other as Grandpa prepared himself for work. He was about to leave when he noticed Craig making his way to the bathroom looking extremely pale and withdrawn, and even though he had cause for concern, Grandpa knew he had responsibilities to fulfil at work.

As the morning passed, Grandpa found it impossible to focus on his duties and with concerns for Craig occupying his mind he made a decision which would later prove to be one of great foresight and divine intervention.

He made his way home for lunch, which was something he had never done before. When he arrived home Grandpa went straight to the boys' bedroom, where he knew Craig would be. He opened the door to find Craig lying lifeless on his back, gasping for air. His back was arched and his face was blue. Grandpa called for Gran to phone an ambulance and she dialled the number frantically while Grandpa, calling on all of his past experience and training as a master mariner, began to administer CPR. As if by slow motion he continued CPR for what seemed a lifetime, yet with trembling hands he persevered.

Suddenly Craig began coughing and spluttering followed by quick short breaths. His heart began to beat that beat, the sign of life they had been hoping for.

When the ambulance arrived, paramedics carried out further observations of Craig's condition before deciding to fly him south from Shetland by air ambulance to the Royal Infirmary in Aberdeen.

The newly constructed stretch of road leading north via Tingwall airport will always be regarded by my family as 'Craig's road' because his ambulance was the first vehicle to use it. Craig had unofficially opened the new road.

As Grandpa stood on the runway he breathed the fresh Shetland air before boarding the plane. He realised Craig still was not 'out of the woods'.

At home in the Scottish Borders, Mum received the news of Craig's illness and left for Aberdeen immediately. Dad, however, was to have a much more memorable journey. He was working on an oil tanker in the North Sea where the adverse weather conditions stopped him from being directly airlifted. Therefore he chose to risk his life by leaping from a small motorboat onto the leg of a nearby oilrig and with the waves crashing around him, he climbed the ladder to safety on the platform above. He was then airlifted to Aberdeen.

Craig remained in a coma for almost a week as our family held vigil, praying for him to wake. Suddenly, and without warning, Craig awoke and cried out for Gran. He still believed he was in Shetland. To this day there has been no official diagnosis for Craig's illness.

The man we call Grandpa is actually no blood relative but through his act of great intuitive foresight he will always be regarded as our real grandfather. He was the right man, in the right place, at the right time. He married the right woman, and all of his lifetime of decisions had led him here, and at this moment he chose to stand up and be counted. He saved Craig's life and for this we will always be grateful.

They say that blood is thicker than water but in this case actions speak louder than words. Death or permanent brain damage occurs when the body is without an airway for more than ten minutes, so the fact that Grandpa arrived home unexpectedly at precisely the right moment is proof enough to me that God was at work that day.

'There's no such thing as God,' my friend had insisted, but I knew he was wrong.

At one time most of my family believed, but as the years passed they frequently lost faith. Even Craig found a period in his life when he no longer believed. Whenever doubt creeps in or I lose faith, I remind myself of that day, and of the culmination of events which led to Grandpa saving Craig's life.

A QUIET HERO
Margaret Bull

HE SHIVERED IN the cold air of the early morning as he pulled on his clothes, avoiding shoving his arm through the hole in the elbow of his jumper, folding the holes in his socks under his feet and cursing when he realised his tackety bits hadn't dried out from the night before. The gentle rhythmic snoring of the family sounded al around him as he pulled on his jacket and bunnet and stepped out of the door. Aye it wiz guid tae ken he'd be back sin fur some breakfast when Maggie wid be up and hud the fire gan weel.

The air was real nippy as he headed out crook in hand to go and check the lambs next tae the hoose and see that they had survived the night. He felt very tired and worn but there was never much time for sleeping at lambing time. The fermer wasnae happy at a' that there had been ower mony deed lambs this season but wit wud cud ye dae in a hard wunter like this ane had been sae fer!

'Aw! Bugger,' whit wiz this? Anither youw layin' deid an' twae wee lambies shiverin' wi' cauld bit still hud breath in them. It wa a rush back tae the hoose but quicker than gan oot because o' the urgency o' the situation.

'Maggie, Maggie set thae auld secks at the fire an see tae these weans. Be quick an fix them up wei some milk tae.' Maggie rushed around following his demands, hair flying everywhere, no time to tie it back!

Off he went again tae attend his flock while the family attended to their life-saving administrations.

This short story is a minuscule glimpse into the life of my grand father and his family. He was born and lived for most of his life in the lonely Lammermuir Hills working as a hill shepherd. He was born to a father who was a shepherd.

Their home was tied to their work so everything was dependent on how well his job was done. The family home was typical of farm workers homes at that time and was shared with his parents and the children. It was a stone cottage well out on its own and the children had a round trip of eight miles to walk to attend the nearest village school. The floors of the house were laid with cement blocks and were somewhat uneven so dirt escaped from between them. The only heating was the open fire and cooking was done on the 'swee' which hung over the fire.

Water was obtained from a spring on the hillside and carted to the house. The only toilet facility was a dry toilet which had to be emptied into a trench daily.

Washing was done by boiling water over the fire then carting it outside and washing with a scrubbing board.

He had not always been on the farm but had also spent time in the King's Own Scottish Borderers and served in Hong Kong where he met with an accident. He was run over by a truck and his arm was crushed. He should have lost his arm but an innovative army surgeon inserted a metal plate in his arm and the arm functioned well after. He was part of the military police in Hong Kong.

He was a man whom I never saw raise his voice. When asked a question he would light his pipe and sit and consider before answering. He always seemed to have a wise reply. He encouraged me greatly to get an education and when I wanted to study nursing he purchased me a nurse's watch two years early!

In his 50s he developed heart problems and had many heart attacks but he would recover and get back to work which was at that time as a petrol pump attendant. When he died in his early 60s he was very sadly missed.

Some years later when I was struggling with exams I was sitting in my bedroom studying and feeling hopeless when a strong smell of tobacco pervaded the room.

It smelt like Grampa's pipe tobacco and all of a sudden I understood the book I was reading. I passed the exam with distinction. I cannot explain that but am left wondering!

He was a quiet man who went about his life with dignity and who made a difference in the life of others but was probably hardly noticed. He worked hard and honestly all his life without complaint. This to me is the mark of a true hero. My hero! My grandfather!

THE SNIPER WHO CAME TO TEA

Murray Peebles

GRANNY PEEBLES LIVED in a state of fear. Make sure it's a strong-looking train before you get on it. Don't use the bathroom taps after I've gone to bed. Your pavements are going to ruin my shoes. Don't visit me when my Home Help's here or they'll think I don't need her to come. If I miss the bus I'll miss *Blind Date*. Kenneth, I think I've been shot –

* * *

Granny and Grampa lived in a flat in Perth Road, Dundee, up a closie between a sweetie shop and a bank. What could be better than having a sweetie shop downstairs from your grandparents' flat? But for Granny, what could be worse than having children using taps unsupervised when the bank manager's office was directly below your bathroom? Imagine if we had flooded not just the bank, but the office of the manager of the Royal Bank of Scotland!

Whenever we visited their flat, the first thing I always did was to challenge Grampa to a game of Connect Four. The result wasn't too important; the novelty of the purple and green discs of Grampa's home-made version was enough for me. Afterwards, Grampa would wind his watch and set the time according to Ceefax, before putting his coat on and heading outside. Across the road from the flat, there was an empty plot of land with a couple of wooden benches where he went to smoke. Behind the benches stood a large billboard, facing right into my grandparents' living room. If this was targeted advertising, then it was preaching to the converted. Grampa didn't need a second invitation to Come to Marlboro Country. From the window of the flat I would watch him lighting up, a grey, huddled figure dwarfed by the tanned cowboy tending to his campfire.

Grampa worked as a joiner in the family business, eventually taking over when my great grandfather retired. In 1965, by then in his mid-50s, Grampa decided on a change of career. He sold the business and became a violin teacher. My older brothers and my cousins had lessons from Grampa, but I didn't. Perhaps by the time

I was old enough, he was too old, or too infirm. Grampa died when I was eight, so there are many things that I never had the chance to speak to him about. His watercolours, painted in the '50s, offer a fascinating glimpse of his wartime service in India and Burma, but I'd love to be able to go back and hear about it first-hand.

Granny outlived Grampa by almost a decade, so my recollections of her are much sharper. I can still see the little splits in her earlobes, the result of years of wearing heavy earrings. She always wore the same perfume, Giorgio Beverly Hills apparently, a distinctive scent that now seems incongruous whenever I encounter anyone under the age of 70 wearing it. When you gave Granny a hug, you would feel the brush of her soft permed hair on your cheek, and if, like me, you were wearing glasses, there would be an inevitable clinking together of frames. Granny's favourite television programme (other than *Blind Date*) was the snooker. She would watch it for hours on end, peering through her outsized octagonal lenses, like Dennis Taylor himself, studying the table at the Crucible.

* * *

In the '70s, Dad started making home-brew wine. This involved much trial and error, probably cancelling out any financial benefits, but eventually he hit upon a successful formula. The precious vintage was bottled, sealed and stored away in the wine cellar. By cellar, I mean the rack of horizontal bottles he'd placed along the top of the kitchen cupboards, and by sealed, I mean that corks were forced into the necks of the bottles and prayers said. One summer Sunday afternoon, Granny and Grampa came for tea. A bottle of the dubious elixir was almost certainly consumed, although it's doubtful whether the ever-cautious Granny could have been persuaded to partake. In the end though, she didn't have a choice; her fate was sealed the minute she sat down facing the kitchen cupboards, beneath the massed ranks of the wine-bottle cannonry.

* * *

The day Granny thought she'd been shot is a story told time and again. Its passage into family legend is not just down to the inherent comedy of the incident, but also the irony of safety-conscious

Granny unwittingly placing herself in such jeopardy. The pop of the cork escaping the bottle, the dull thud as it struck the wall next to Granny's head, the arc of red wine homing in on her white blouse and, of course, her startled reaction to the one eventuality that even she couldn't have foreseen – these are things that none of us will ever forget. And yet, it was only recently, when I asked my parents to recall everything they could of that day, that I discovered it took place before I was even born. 'No, no, we were buying wine by the time you came along,' said Dad, instantly dismissing my protestations. At first I felt ashamed about all the times I've told this story as if I had been there, but on reflection I don't feel so bad. The boundary between true stories and family legends has always been a blurred line.

WHAT TO TELL THE GRANDCHILDREN

Douglas Forrest

SO, HOW DO I break it to the grandchildren? The first part is the hardest. I have to extricate them from a wide assortment of electronic gadgetry. 'Hey kids, did you know you've got a famous antecedent?'

'A what? Like what's an anti-whatsit?'

'Antecedent, don't they teach you anything at school these days?'

Eyes roll. 'Cut to the chase Granddad.'

'Okay, did you know that your great grandfather had a famous uncle?'

'Cool. What did he do?'

'He's had books written about him.'

'Great, can we see the DVD?'

'Oh come on. Get real. Not every book gets made into a film. Some stories are only available in books. This is one of them.'

'So what was he then? Was he a soldier? Did he win loads of medals?'

'Not exactly, but he was shot at by Tibetan monks with bows and arrows once. He was with a party of 17 others. The monks killed all the other people. He was the only one who survived.'

'Why didn't he shoot them with his gun?'

'He couldn't. He didn't have any guns.'

'I thought monks were holy men. Why were they shooting at him if he wasn't a soldier?'

'These monks were different. They were warrior monks and they didn't like foreigners coming into their country. They would kill them and they would also kill anyone who had helped them. They weren't very nice people.'

'Wow, so how did he escape?'

'He had to go along fast-flowing streams after dark and hide up in the daytime. He travelled many miles like this. He almost died of starvation. He was eventually rescued by some Chinese farmers. He was really lucky. You know all that happened to him when they were attacked was that he had two arrows through his hat.'

'Well, if he wasn't a soldier what was he doing amongst Tibetan monks? Was he a famous explorer like Livingstone?'

'Er, not exactly, though he went back to China six more times.'

'Go on, tell us. What did he do?'

'He was born in Scotland, in the town of Falkirk. That was away back in 1873. When he left school he became an apprentice chemist.'

'Did he make explosives?'

'No, he learnt about plants. You see in those days it was known that certain plants could be used to help cure illnesses. The plants had to be dried in a special way before medicines could be made from them. He was taught how to do this.'

'Did he go and tell the Chinese how to make medicine?'

'No, you see the Chinese were the first people known to have discovered the medicinal properties of plants. But he did something to help them as far as medicine is concerned.'

'What was that?'

'With his own money he paid to have many poor Chinese children inoculated against smallpox. He saved lots of lives that way.'

'Sounds like he was a good guy.'

'Yes, we all share his genes so that is why we are all so good, isn't it?'

'But that doesn't explain how he came to be in China in the first place, Granddad.'

'No, you're quite right. Mind you China wasn't the first overseas place he went to.'

'Okay, so where did he go?'

'When he was still at the chemist's shop he was left some money in a will. With it he bought a ticket to Australia. He set himself up as a sheep farmer. He thought he'd make his fortune out there and even went gold prospecting.'

'Wow, Granddad! Did he get really rich? Was he a millionaire who spent his money travelling?'

'Not exactly, it all went pear-shaped. He had to give up those dreams and come back home.'

'What was his name? Was he really famous like Bill Gates?'

'His name was George Forrest. I don't expect you've heard of him.'

'Nope! Can't be that famous.'

'You could try and Google it.'

Experienced fingers rattle across keyboards. The penny drops.

'Granddad, he was a plant collector. How utterly girly is that?'

They take off like startled birds. I call after them, 'He collected over 10,000 previously undiscovered varieties of plants and has had many of them named after him.' My words are drowned by the sound of a Ford Mustang roaring down Interstate 21 hotly pursued by a blacktop with its siren wailing.

With a sigh I sit back. 'I'm going to create a video game where the character is George the plant collector and you get points for every new species you discover. Do you think it will catch on?'

THE PRICE OF FISH

Diane Kearns

'YERRA RAKE, like yer father!' Grandad couldn't sit still for long and had walked off to look at the sea. I'd been sent to tow him back to the family party and these were the puzzling words that greeted him, puzzling because he wasn't tall and thin. Grandad was called Purse and had one with a tray into which he could shake his coins. 'I can count my bawbies now,' he'd wink at me, knowing this would provoke Grandma again: 'Yer Scotch tight, just like yer father!'

At the first family do of a new year, Grandad would toast us: 'Lang may yer lungs reek, as my Da would say.' I thought we were well on course as all the grownups smoked like chimneys. He'd drink tea at these gatherings: 'I signed up to the suns o' temprance when I was young,' he'd explain, the concept of Grandad's youth as mystifying to me as the strange phrase. 'Yer've never been a boozer, Purse, like yer father,' Grandma would say fondly, and add, 'He liked his Scotch did his father – it's the price of fish.' So here was a presence around which my family spun myths; who was Scotch and liked it, tight, boozy, a reeking rake.

As I grew up words were heard less bafflingly, perhaps because I became a keen reader. When I graduated to Grandad's collection of boys' adventure stories, my appreciation of Henty, Ballantyne, Stevenson, prompted fragmentary tales of his own. Grandad's father had bought the books; he was a mariner, often long away from home, who arrived back flush – if the gods had been good – with bawbies and Scotch, the legend of his leathery hands keeping a growing family of sons in check. He had started on the sailboats, fishing out of Fife only a little older than I was then. He was a deckie, tidying, hauling, furling, cutting and coiling. Any metal and his fingers would freeze to it in cold weather, which was nine months of the year in Scotland. Lines would ice up and topple a boat as if it were a bath toy; a rope left untidied would slip and tip a man into the sea, sea so cold it would stop your heart in seconds.

Percy (I now knew Grandad's name) and his brothers weren't allowed to learn to swim; swimming only prolonged the time before drowning. Two brothers did go out to sea but Grandad had been the bookish one at the fireside with his adventure writers, although Da's tales were as good as anything printed: with the advent of steam trawling he had become an engineer and joined the big boats raking up round Iceland for the prize catches. As a young man he had seen polar bears and been nearly capsized by a whale's fluke. In summer the light never faded and in winter ice covered the decks and icebergs sang, while emerald and citrine streaked the sky overhead. He brought back bone carved into knotwork, a legendary worm eating itself with no beginning or end. Carving helped his crew to relax, for once on duty modern machinery could rip a man apart with a moment's inattention, but this was the price of fish.

Now I'm approaching Grandad Percy's age and have started trawling memories for family history. This man, delineated only through phrases and stories, now has a title: Great Grandfather. He now has a name: James Thompson. I hold his marriage certificate but there is no guarantee his stated age or paternal details are true. Yet the fantastic tales of northern waters I can believe now – this was how food was put on the table at a time when labourers bent double in the fields and stockboys herded in bare feet.

The four censuses after his marriage tell of his brood increasing and living in various ports along Britain's east coast, a family anchored by my great grandmother, always carefully describing herself as a 'Marine Engineer's Wife'. He was alive but never at home, at least not at census time; did he stay onshore for long, or was the sea his real habitat; was this choice, or was it the price of fish? Was he from Fife; did he enjoy a drink; was he careful with money, or is this all family taradiddle? James Thompson, who left such an uncommon impression on his descendents and who had such a common name he is impossible to trace, has become as slippery and unquantifiable – except as the subject of legend – as the fish he once chased.

MERCY BOO COO

Catherine Simpson

GRAN WAS LIKE Robinson Crusoe; a solitary survivor, an unkempt outsider, a one-off. For a start, Gran was a man.

It didn't seem strange. We were used to saying 'Gran needs more baccy for his pipe,' or 'Gran's having a shave.'

Instead of a tropical island, Gran had washed up in the old dairy where his wife used to make cheese. I call her his wife because she died years before I was born and we never knew her as anything; her name was never mentioned.

By the 1970s the cheese shelves were packed with the flotsam and jetsam of his farming life: decoy ducks, old milk bottles, Tilley lamps, rolls of wire. Pushed up against them was his armchair, ingrained with grime and packed with newspapers where the springs used to be. He had a black and white television, a huge wireless and a stack of westerns from the mobile library.

Bit by bit the dairy filled up with broken furniture that my mother wouldn't have in the house: legless chairs, chairless dining tables, over-wound clocks and a wooden fire-surround. Gran kept anything that had been his wife's; slowly surrounding himself with tangled junk, all settling to a dusty gray.

A two-bar electric fire kept him warm along with a pig lamp dangling from the ceiling and shining on his white hair. The farm cats slept around his shoulders, sharing his lamp. When one of the cats died on a sofa in there, another cat flattened the body and turned it into a bed before anyone noticed.

At mealtimes Gran came into the farmhouse to eat, shuffling in his slippers across the yard to see what was on offer. If it had a crust or a hard skin he'd go back for his false teeth. He ate all his meals off a single plate, wiping it clean between courses with a slice of bread and butter. He ate everything: fat, gristle, the lot. If we grimaced he'd say 'You lot, you don't know you're born.'

After the meal he'd gather any scraps and take them out for the cats. They waited for him in a yowling semicircle and as he selected which morsels to drop, they climbed up each leg and clung to his chest, shouting in his face.

On our birthdays he gave us 50 pence. He rooted through his pockets, sorting handfuls of washers and bits of straw until he found one. He chuckled dryly as he handed it over. Life was tough and we'd better get used to it.

He was a veteran of the trenches at Ypres where he was shot through the shoulder. He was taken to hospital in Boulogne where he learned to thank the nurses – mercy boo coo.

As an old man his war was with moles. He carried a pen knife for slicing apples, shredding baccy, paring his nails and resetting his mole traps. He walked the farm wearing an old mack tied round with baling twine, chewing baccy and checking his traps. He was vigilant for signs of invasion; constantly on the look out for soil explosions where the moles had broken cover from their underground trenches. Then, along the trench, he'd set the sturdy metal trap with the ferocious grip. When he caught one he'd leave it dead in the field to be scavenged by the crows and the foxes.

One day a mole crossed the farmyard and plunged into his seedling tray.

'Gran! Your lettuces are moving.'

We watched as the seedlings erupted from the tray one by one. Gran emerged from his dairy.

'Kill it.'

We dived on the tray and dragged the mole to safety. Gran spat out his tobacco in disgust and the dog ate it.

'You lot, you don't know you're born.'

* * *

My school project was to 'Interview a grandparent and find out what life was like many years ago'. I went out to the old dairy.

'Gran, I need to know about the olden days.'

He was sunk deep in his armchair with his legs crossed. He took out his baccy pouch and rooted around for his pen knife.

'What did you do on a Sunday?'

Gran shredded his baccy into a neat pile. I stood, pencil poised as the silence grew. He took his pipe and scraped the bowl with his pen knife; round and round.

'Put on me fustian breeches,' he banged the pipe on his chair arm, 'and watched tide come in, 'appen.'

My pencil hovered over my exercise book. I wrote 'Watched tide' and looked at it.

'But Gran, what did you do for fun?'

'Fun?' He chuckled a bit and tamped baccy down in his pipe-bowl; shoving it in with his thumbnail. Then he struck a match and sucked as the baccy flared orange. He closed his eyes and said nothing.

'What did you do in the war, then, Gran?'

Gran took his pipe out of his mouth and examined it. It had gone out. He pushed in more baccy.

'War... huh.' He struck another match and sucked. The match went out and he tried again as I shuffled from foot to foot.

'War.' He puffed hard then laid his head back and shut his eyes again. 'You lot,' he gave another puff, 'you don't know you're born.'

I stood in silence for a minute then closed my notebook and edged towards the door.

'Okay, Gran. Thanks.'

A wisp of smoke coiled from his pipe as he took it from the corner of his mouth but he didn't open his eyes.

'Mercy boo coo.'

THE MINISTER, THE PIRATE
AND THE PRIVATE

Elizabeth Copp

MY GRANDFATHER'S GREAT, great uncle was a pirate. Now there's a conversation-stopper if ever there was one. I found this out by chance some 30 years after my grandfather, Creighton Allan, died peacefully in Orkney at the age of 83, and 160 years after his ancestral uncle, Robert Creighton Bryden, was hanged in the East Indies. Did the young Creighton know about Robert's fate? Probably not. Those were the days when family skeletons were locked up and the key thrown away. Will I offend my ancestors if I resurrect this piratical ghost? I hope not. There is good and bad in all of us and there must be some of Robert's blood in my veins along with that of my grandfather's.

This story begins with two photographs. You see, I wasn't actually looking for Robert – I was searching for my grandfather's past.

In an old family album I came across 25901 Private William Creighton Allan – 15 Platoon, 9th Gordon Highlanders. He was aged 18. He was a quiet sensitive man, yet there he is standing in uniform, second from the right, about to leave for the horrors of the trenches. He made it back home by chance. They say that in life you make your own choices and consequently your own luck, but I don't think that applied in the Great War. He was just lucky, end of story. He survived Ypres while thousands were slaughtered and afterwards somehow avoided death while marching to God-knows-where. The man in front of him was killed, the man behind had his leg blown off, while he himself escaped with shrapnel in his finger. That shrapnel saved him, for he was sent to hospital and didn't go back to the Front. Had he not been the man in the middle, I wouldn't be writing this story.

Then I turned a page of the album to see a portrait of a rather gloomy minister. 'That's a face to frighten the bairns and horses,' said a friend, drily. I had to agree. By now I was intrigued, for no-one had mentioned this august character in our family. So I trawled the archives and – eureka! I had found my four times great grand-father, John Glendinning Bryden, who had travelled from Dumfries with his young bride to become a minister in Shetland in the early 19th century. That seems to me pretty impressive. To travel across Scotland before roads were macadamised and railways had opened takes a bit of planning. And how long did the journey by steamer from Leith to Shetland take? This was not a voyage for the faint-hearted.

They had three daughters and then a son, Robert Creighton Bryden, born in 1825. And there under his name on a genealogical website were the words 'Hanged for piracy in the East Indies before 1851.' How must that feel, to have a longed-for son die a lonely death overseas after committing a crime?

So why did Robert fall from grace when he had parents who had mettle and determination? Had he inherited his parents' sense of adventure and wanted to travel far? A Dutch East Indiaman had been lost with all hands in a storm off Shetland a century before he had been born. Silver ducatoons and some gold coins were to be washed ashore years later. Perhaps Robert had his own legend to seek and had worked his passage east on a similar sailing ship, lured by the promise of wealth. Then maybe he had simply been in the wrong place at the wrong time, unlike my grandfather to whom the Fates were kind. After all, Sir Francis Drake was regarded by the Spanish as a pirate while being feted by the establishment in England.

Or is this a classic case of the elder son of the manse rebelling against a strict sabbatical regime? In those days, the Sabbath was strictly for rest, worship and Bible study. John Glendinning Bryden stuck to these sabbatical rules and insisted that they were upheld. I know this, because records show that he wrote a statement in 1849 regarding the profanation of the Sabbath by three Shetland fisherman who had gone hunting for whales. There is no doubt he would have insisted on similar standards at home. Ironically, it could well have been around this same time that Robert was hanged for piracy. There are rules to be obeyed in any society and Robert had broken them. He paid a harsh price.

So which of these three men, all from the same blood-line, is the legend? Is it the minister, who travelled the length of Scotland to a far-flung parish in the Northern Isles? Or his son, the pirate – surely a classic case of a legend if ever there was one? Or my grand-father, the private, who survived the Great War and came back to Orkney to live and work quietly in the community? He fell in love with my grandmother and they were married for nearly 60 years. He became mechanic-in-charge of Post Office vehicles in 1929 in Kirkwall and stayed in that post until his retirement in 1960. It was an ordinary life, to be honest.

Then on his retirement, my grandfather was awarded the Imperial Service Medal in recognition of '... the invaluable work he had done' in that post and for '... zealous and conscientious service'. He was surprised to be honoured.

I've chosen my family legend. I'll let you make your own choice.

THE STAR OF THE FAMILY

Ann MacLaren

I NEVER REALLY knew my great grandmother. I couldn't have been more than three when she died, but I always thought of her as a bit of a star. She was the family 'character', the one all the stories were told about. My father, mother, aunts and uncles, all had a tale to tell about Great Granny. It seemed to me as a child that everyone had known her but myself. Even my sister, who was a few years older than me, was lucky enough to have been witness to Great Granny falling out of bed drunk once, and was able to create her own myth about the incident.

The stories about Great Granny were always funny and most revolved around drink. She liked her whisky, no – loved her whisky. Apparently she never went out without a quarter bottle of the amber nectar in her handbag, and was known to offer a drink to her fellow passengers when she took the tram three stops along the road to get her shopping. She was quite crafty too when she had no money to buy a drink: she once offered to do a shopping for a neighbour – to save her legs, she said – and came back a couple of hours later with a bone and a couple of coppers in change, telling the neighbour, 'I thought you might fancy making a pot of soup.'

Great Granny was one of the few women who frequented the pubs close to where she lived, and was always delighted when any strangers came into these establishments because it gave her the opportunity to tell them, 'It's my birthday today, son. I'm 90.'

She was in her late 70s by this stage, but she probably looked 90. The men, of course, always bought her a drink.

Not long before she died, when she was living with my grandparents, she went missing one night, and my grandfather was sent to look for her. He knew if he did the rounds of the pubs in the area he would eventually find her, and sure enough there she was, about two miles from home, in a hostelry where nobody knew her, propped up at the bar. He tried to persuade her to come home, and when he took hold of her arm to help her off the stool she began to scream and cry, shouting that she was being attacked, that this man was trying to abduct her. My grandfather fled – just in case anyone was inclined to believe her.

How we all used to laugh at these tales of a silly old woman addicted to her daily tipple. All except my grandmother that is. She was the only person who seemed to have no story to tell about Great Granny. When I became aware of this as I was growing up, I assumed it was because she didn't like the idea of her own mother being made fun of. Later, I wondered if it was because she herself was very much against strong drink, and didn't approve of her mother's glorification through alcohol.

But not long before she died she did eventually tell me a 'Great Granny' story. She told me how she had grown up in abject poverty because of her mother's drinking habit. Her father worked all the hours he could to try to give the family a decent standard of living, but much of his hard-earned cash went to the local publican. The whole family often went hungry, and they never knew what it was to have new clothes. When the time came for my grandmother, the oldest child, to take her first communion, her mother had spent the money she had promised to save for the special white dress – on whisky. So my granny had to line up with all the other little girls in their pretty white confections wearing a brown school frock, the only dress she owned.

'But I forgave her,' said my granny. 'She was my mother.'

So now I know that, although she provided us all with much entertainment, and although the family laughed and joked and handed down stories that created the legend that was my great grandmother, it was my granny who was the real star.

Childhood Legends

GALLUSES

Celia Craig

THIS TRUE STORY has become one of Gurden's myths. It was told to me by my father who doubtless heard it first-hand or from a family member. It has always made me burst out laughing.

Jim was looking forward to his birthday, his tenth birthday and his first appearance in his new breeks, lang breeks. Nae mair reid, frosted knees. It was still cauld for Merch and lang breeks would be just the ticket. Only twa days to go and he could join the ranks of the big laddies and torment the wee laddies aboot their short breeks.

As he ran up to the school he spied his cousin, Alex Craig, already in lang breeks.

'Aye, Alex, hiv ye feenished sheelin yir mither's mussels this morning?'

Alex grinned at him. 'Aye, didna taak lang, Jim,' he replied, 'but Jeems hisna near din his jar yet and Wullie hisna started.' Alex's sister, Lizzie, was excused from the daily sheelin but had a number of household chores to do instead.

They sprinted the last few yards together. Jim did not have to contribute to this chore in his family, the chore of sheelin a jar of mussels for your mother before you went to school to help her out, with the task of baiting the 1,200-hook line with two, even three mussels per hook. This would allow her to carry on baiting, rather than stopping to shell more and more mussels for the non-ending line, itself a long and wearisome job, till rows and rows of baited hooks lay neat and tidy in the long basket skull that would be shot off the stern of the boat next day by his father to fish for the cod and haddock that comprised the family's living. Jim's father worked in the village flax mill though his granny came from a fishing family.

The day of Jim's birthday dawned bright and sunny which was just as well, for after school Jim would carry out the delightful task of visiting each of his close relatives in turn to get his birthday presents. He looked down at his new serge breeks happily. They were maybe a wee bittie ower lang and kitly but they were a rare colour, navy blue. He was hoping for a new gansey to match by the time he had been round everybody. It was unlikely that his gansey would be trimmed with three pearl buttons at the side of the neck as ganseys for adults were but he could hope.

'Faur are ye gaen first, Jim?' shouted Alex as he cantered past doon the brae on his way home for a piece of loaf and syrup after school.

'Startin at the Back Street wi mi Auntie Merge and mi Auntie Mysie, then doon Bridge Street to the herber and Auntie Mag, through the toon and doon Moowatt's Lane and alang East End ti Aikey's and back up the Lane to Arbuthnott Street and Mootie's.'

Alex nodded. Mootie was his mother, Liz Mowatt, Mrs Craig.

'Mibbe see ye at the hoose in a whilie then!' cried Alex. 'Yir new breeks are smashin and mi mither his a richt gid present fir ye that'll match yir breeks. Hey, I think I can see the *Craigielea* and mi father comin in fae the sea. Cheerio.'

Jim cast his eyes over the sea towards the horizon and sure enough spotted the boat heading for Gurden harbour where he could see the boats that had already returned, proudly moored, over 20-, 30- and 40-footers stretching right across the harbour. However, by the time Jim reached the harbour he was a little daunted. After a visit to Mag Wyllie's the feeling had deepened but he carried carefully in his hand three small boxes containing his birthday presents. Certainly his new breeks had been much admired which was some consolation.

'Fa's gotten new lang breeks then?'

The sudden cry startled Jim out of his reverie. He had forgotten the band of fishermen and skippers that congregated at the foot of Bridge Street just up from the harbour to blether and exchange stories and incidents from the day at sea and to tantalise one another with carefully disguised hints about when they might set out for sea the next morning, whether they would rise early to catch high tide or wait till later in hope of a better daylight catch or even tide the boat doon so as to get out nearer low tide when the water in the harbour would be too shallow to float the boat unless it was right down at the mouth of the harbour.

'My, that's a richt pair!' shouted another man and chortled.

'Is it yir birthday or his yir mither won a sweepie?'

Soon several voices could be heard tormenting and teasing Jim who blushed and said 'Aye' and ran on past as fast as possible.

Arriving at Arbuthnott Street after a quick and dispiriting visit to Aikey's, Jim chapped on the door of number 16. Mootie opened the door right away and wished Jim a happy birthday, handing him a small box, his present.

Jim looked at it in dismay.

Holding up four identical boxes, he burst out crying.

'Nae galluses, Mootie!'

'Na, it's nae galluses, Jim,' said Mootie. 'It's a belt! But three pairs'll come in affy handy or ye kid aye start a shoppie!'

PATRICIA'S CHAIR

Mari O'Brien

AS SOON AS I saw her, I knew she wasn't a 'Melody'. Throughout the nine months leading up to the arrival of my third child, our chosen names had been rigidly set but there was something in her dainty features, green eyes and auburn hair that made us reassess this. As well as the screaming. The only way I can describe it is angry. Angry screaming. Yes, we knew immediately that she wasn't going to be the girly girl we had always imagined. 'Melody' was too girly, too sickly sweet. Our daughter was most definitely a Pattie. Everything about her instantly reminded me of my Auntie Pat.

I am not one of those people who can vividly recall their childhood but there was one person whom I remember fondly. My Auntie Pat, like Pattie, was born in Glasgow, but almost seventy years earlier. My father's sister, she never married, and lived with my uncle in the Scotstoun area of Glasgow. I grew up in Aberdeen with my parents and older sister. It was the 1980s and my father worked as an engineer on the oil rigs and wasn't around a lot, but when he was, we used to make the long car journey down to Glasgow to visit his siblings for a few days.

On one occasion my parents left my sister and I in the care of my aunt and uncle while they went on a short holiday to London. On arriving at their house we all sat together for a while in the lounge. I remember Auntie Pat, immaculately dressed in a pencil skirt and mohair jumper, entering the room. She placed an enormous circular tin of Roses chocolates on the coffee table to the horror of my strict and controlling, yet loving, mother who did not agree with giving children sugary treats. Being a cheeky child, I secretly enjoyed watching my mother's face as I devoured handfuls of chocolates one after another, the purple ones being my favourite. 'That's enough now,' my mum said, politely through clenched teeth. Auntie Pat and I exchanged knowing glances with each other.

The next day, I remember sitting on the front row of a double-decker bus on the way to Whiteinch Park with Auntie Pat and my sister. It was a glorious, hot, summer's day, as they always seem to be in my memories.

'Let's get you two a couple of cans of juice when we get there,' my aunt said. 'It's boiling.'

'My mum doesn't let us have fizzy drinks,' came my sister's reply.

'Your mum's bum!' Auntie Pat declared, 'I'm looking after you today.' I was so shocked I didn't know what to say. Sandwiched between the two, I looked up at Auntie Pat who was looking straight ahead. I couldn't see her face behind all that red hair, glistening in the sun. Then she nudged me and I knew she was smiling. I smiled too. My poor sister, her mouth remained wide open for the continuation of the bus ride.

That evening, as I lay on the makeshift bed on the floor of my aunt's room, next to my sleeping sister, I propped myself up on my elbows and surveyed the room. I couldn't sleep. With its 1950s furniture, red, swirling, patterned carpet and brown wallpaper, I desperately wanted the familiarity of my own bedroom. And my mum. I slowly descended the stairs. Through the darkness, I could see a small light was on in the kitchen as the door was ajar. I tiptoed into the room and found my aunt sitting in a white rocking chair, lost in thought.

'I miss my mum,' I whispered. She jumped slightly but ushered me over to her. 'Come here, silly girl,' she said, her bright green eyes smiling at me. I fell asleep in her arms that night.

I have a wonderful memory of Auntie Pat singing 'I'm Forever Blowing Bubbles' while she bathed my sister and I. The bath water was freezing cold but the bubbles, laughter and singing made up for it. She also taught us how to dance, rock and roll style to The Beatles. We didn't dance much at home, and being pretty quiet and reserved children, we awkwardly swayed along to the music. 'Move your hips!' she would shout at us, laughing, her wild red hair flying around. Everything was so different to what I was used to at home. There was no order or routine. Our meals were simple and usually cold and we were given as much sweets and ice cream as we could possibly eat. On our last day there, while my mother and father loaded up the car, she took me by the hand to the kitchen.

'See the next time you come over, you can help me paint this,' she said, pointing to a white, tired-looking rocking chair in the corner of the room, 'okay?'

'Okay,' I said.

We never did paint the chair. That was the last time I ever saw her.

I was eight when she passed away on 11 January 1989, aged 48. Years later I was told she died of liver failure. It was only then that everything began to make sense. When we went to visit she would often disappear for hours at a time, and it was only ever my uncle who came to visit us in Aberdeen. I would sometimes overhear concerned, whispered conversations between my parents and my uncle during his time spent with us. I would never question it though, I was too young.

Pattie celebrated her first birthday on 12 December 2008. On helping her open a large package from a friend, I was surprised to come across a small, white, child's chair. It also contained a box of paints. Pattie, along with her two older brothers and I, painted the chair with bright colours and her name P A T T I E on the back. While listening to The Beatles.

NELLIE'S SPECIAL CHITTERING BITE

Elaine Renton

GRAN TOOK ME TO The Baths early every Sunday. Sitting on the bus up to Falkirk, I would be sick with anticipation, and when I finally smelt the chlorine filtering out of the ugly red building, I was sure that it was possible to die of excitement.

Gran lined her drawers and shelves with old newspapers, and to this day the combination of newsprint and the sharp smell of old varnish reminds me of swimming Sundays.

There was a heavy, oak chest of drawers at one side of Gran's bed. The clothes I kept at her house were all in the bottom drawer and my drawer was the one that stuck the most, swollen with damp. I would have to jerk at the brass handles until the drawer gave way, inch by inch, and I could reach my swimming costume. It was a turquoise ruched affair, and as I grew, the fish-scale effect of the ruches disappeared as the material stretched, accommodating my unsettling new body.

Even if the pool was empty, Gran would insist that we shared a changing cubicle. We would walk along the white and black, chipped tiles and stop at the same cubicle every week, right up at the deep end, under the big clock. Gran liked that particular cubicle, because the spectators up in the gallery would have a hard time seeing down past the clock. I never saw any spectators.

Pulling the faded, canvas curtain over the space at the top of the door, Gran got me ready first. She would make me stand up on the wooden seat, slats bleached with decades of chlorinated water dripping from bathing-suited behinds. I had to stand up there, because if I stood on the slippery tiled floor, someone in the pool might see my knickers come down and over my impatient feet.

Personally, the fear of getting a verruca and being banned from the pool worried me more than someone seeing my knickers.

The yellow bathing cap Gran bought me was a manufacturing abomination. To distract the wearer from the fact that it was actually designed as an instrument of torture, the cap was decorated on one side with a giant chrysanthemum, cunningly crafted from orange and white rubber petals.

There was always a kirby grip in Gran's purse, and she would have it at the ready, caught onto her top teeth, twisting my hair into a vicious ponytail and securing it, with the kirby grip, on top of my poor head. Keeping her left hand on the captured hair, Gran would lift the swimming cap from her string bag, and flick it onto my head. She freed her left hand at the last second, leaving the ponytail under the cap, and with both hands, she would yank the sides of the tight cap right down, deftly fastening the chinstrap to the small metal buckle dangling against my cheek.

During my swimming lessons I must have had the look of someone permanently startled, with my eyebrows arched high on my forehead, my scalp pulled up tight by the ponytail.

Before she gave me my weekly lesson, Gran made me stand, fidgeting and fretting, facing the cubicle door, while she removed her shoes and stockings. She would shake her empty stockings, roll them together, and then put them into one shoe. Once my clothes were hidden under a big white towel, she pulled the snib back, letting me loose to cannonball into the deep end, and swim down the length of the pool, to wait for my lesson.

I had been threatened with a thick ear if I ever removed my bathing cap in the water, and an unquestioning child, I did as I was told. However, once I hit the water, the cap would swell and rise, making me look as if I had a massive, egg-shaped skull. The cap only stayed on my head by means of the strap digging hard into my chin, and I would wonder why I had to wear a bathing cap in the first place.

Gran never went into the water and I had never seen her swim. Yet for 20 minutes, I did breadths, backwards and forwards, while she shouted instructions. She would glare daggers at anyone who dared swim in front of me, or worse, got a bit too exuberant and splashed her, sweltering and still wearing her tweed coat at the side of the shimmering pool. Through her expert tuition, I developed a strange but effective, puddock-like stroke, which hauled me through the water at a fair pace.

At the end of my lesson, I was free for half an hour, and that was never long enough for all the surface dives, handstands and roly polys that I was so good at performing for my Gran.

Then out, blue-lipped and shivering, to be stood back up on the wooden bench, stripped and dried vigorously and covered in Cuticura talc. Gran always gave me a bar of chocolate-covered puff candy to eat while she replaced her stockings. She called it Nellie's Special Chittering Bite and only ever bought the proper stuff, made by Ross's. Puff candy was one of the few things she never managed to make herself.

On the way back for the bus, we would nip into the paper shop for *The Sunday Post* and six morning rolls. I could hardly see, red-eyed from the chlorine in the pool, but I was allowed to tear the rolls from the freshly baked soft wads and count them into a paper bag, because Gran knew my hands were clean.

Sometimes, at the bus stop, she would look at the indentation made from the small metal buckle digging into my cheek, feel my wet hair, and tut.

Helen Hastings
1908–1997

HOW OUR GRACE NEARLY DIED
OF THE SCARLET FEVER

Grace Murray

'IT WAS ALL *her father's fault.*'

In 1945 the family lived in a tenement in Paisley. The grownups didn't like us children playing downstairs in the grubby back court so every Saturday morning our father took big sister Margaret (eight) and me (five) to play in the local park while Mother stayed at home to look after the new baby and cook lunch.

We girls treasured these outings. Father let us do all sorts of exciting things, strictly forbidden by Mother. We got to climb the trees and play hide-and-seek in the dense rhododendron shrubbery. He allowed us to paddle in the fountain and scramble onto the fierce, cast iron walruses. He even let us drink from the iron cup chained to the drinking fountain – something we knew perfectly well was prohibited for fear of germs.

Well, when we came home one hot Saturday, mother glanced at our flushed faces and asked, 'Would you like some juice while I dish out?' My big sister kicked my ankle a nanosecond too late and I chirruped, 'No thanks – we had a drink from the fountain.'

Mother froze with upraised ladle, then exploded. How could he have let us do that! Didn't he know there was a killer scarlet fever epidemic raging? We were both doomed! Poor Dad; Margaret and I resolved not to fall ill – or if we did, to suffer bravely in silence so as not to get him in more trouble.

I failed. In a few days, my head and throat began to ache and I was too weak to raise my head, let alone fight the delirium-induced monsters writhing out of the walls. Two ambulance men came and carted me away, clutching Red Rabbity and my cuddly blanket.

What happened to our Grace in hospital.

As soon as I arrived, Sister deemed Red Rabbity and my cuddly blanket unhygienic and wrenched them from my grasp, never to be seen again. Worse, she decided they couldn't possibly care for my cherished long hair and snip-snapped my pigtails off, right up at the scalp.

I cried myself to sleep that night, and every night for the next six weeks. No visiting was allowed in children's wards in those days and no-one ever explained that I would go home when I was better; I thought I had lost my home and family for good.

Legend has it I nearly died of constipation, because I didn't 'go' for weeks. Every morning a nurse would ask, 'Have you had a number two?' I hadn't a clue what that meant, so answered 'Yes' like all the others. When the true state came to light, I was given a glass of castor oil, followed by the most delicious thing in the universe, a finger of Kit Kat – the first chocolate I had ever tasted.

There was another first; I had a real bath in the echoing, white-tiled bathroom. I was thrilled at how my legs floated up in the lovely deep water and confided in the nurses that it was the first bath I'd ever had. Mother was black affronted when she heard, for of course I'd been washed in a tin bath in front of the kitchen fire every week of my life.

My parents were equally distraught at the separation, so Mother's ploy to see me is part of the legend. vj Day occurred – the victory over the Japanese that ended World War ii. Mother baked a celebration cake decorated with tiny, paper Union Jacks and brought it up the hospital. To her dismay, they received it politely, but refused her admission. When Sister showed me the cake, I burst into tears, because Mummy had been so close and not allowed in.

Ward rounds were solemn affairs, with us all on our best behaviour. The wonderful day came when the doctor said I could get up. The second he was gone, I slipped out of bed, only to land in a wailing heap; my legs would no longer support me and I thought I would never walk again. I was scolded for not waiting for help and they marched me up and down the ward till my muscles regained their strength.

Once I was back on my feet, I needed to find the toilets and set off bravely, only to end up in the kitchens by mistake. I whispered my by now urgent need and one of the cooks gestured at a bucket of vegetable peelings. I was scandalised, but a kindlier one of the cooks protested, 'Naw – she's a nice wee thing. Come oan, hen – A'll show you the lavvies.'

Legend has it I ate only toast, custard and my ration of one egg a week all the time I was inside, refusing to eat the lumpy porridge or soggy vegetables. When the nurses insisted, I sicked everything back up. That leads directly on to the final part of the legend.

Mother's astonishing mistake.

One morning Sister said, 'Your mother has arrived to take you home – why don't you go to meet her?' I raced out into the corridor. This lady was approaching who looked very like my mother, carrying a baby who looked very like my little sister, but she sailed on by with nary a glance. I was distraught and ran to sob in the loos. She didn't want me back! Was she going to choose another little girl in my place?

There was general panic till I was found and all was explained. Mother had completely failed to recognise me. She had handed over a plump, confident bundle of mischief and been given back a skeletal, cringing waif. The crowning blow was that I was too weak to walk to the bus stop. She had to pay for a taxi home – an unheard-of luxury that devastated the family budget.

Here endeth the family legend of 'How our Grace nearly died of the scarlet fever.'

COAL MINER'S DOCHTER

Sam Gates

MA THREE SISTERS; Katy and the ither two.

Katy stars in ma very first memory; she's balancing a chip sideways oan a spoon so it turns intae an aeroplane and flees right intae ma mooth, magic!

I was a braw wean, sittin' in ma high-sprung pram surrounded by sisters – till I metamorphosed intae a fat, snottery toddler and the ither two abandoned me. It was Katy who taught me how tae tie ma shoelaces and tell the time, who read tae me and taught me the wee singing rhymes of childhood that stay wae you forever.

And the escapades: I remember her liftin' me up tae pick berries aff the rowan tree, packing them intae pokey hat-shaped bags and selling them at the gate as 'cherries'; anither time – oot guisin' – an auld wummin at the Big Hoose gave us hauf a croon in mistake for tuppence; we ran hame and telt naebody!

As the ither two launched themselves at various innocent boays, I watched as Katy moved intae a different world; she read, she sang, she joined a theatre group in Kilmarnock – and she smiled placidly at the comments the ither two made as she swished aboot in a big dirndl skirt or squeezed intae her snazzy three-quarter length troosers.

I was the youngest – young enough tae feel excluded fae cosy recollections of deid relatives, evacuees fae Glesga and legendary fitba' matches between junior teams wae fanciful names. Mair enjoyable for me were the summer jaunts, winter nights roon the wireless and trips tae the picture hoose. Jeez – that time Katy took me tae see *Jailhouse Rock*! Ma heid reeled for days, still feelin' that beat, still high on the images of jeans, turned up collars and ma first whiff of brash American street life.

Life took oan a new texture! The plain balsa wood of aircraft models paled beside the shiny promise of ma cheap new red guitar; ma beloved *Beanos* looked peely-wally beside the lurid colours of glossy American magazines. I couldnae help myself! I ran, jumped and grabbed at life, high on the swaggerin' confidence of ma musical heroes – wae Katy as ma security net. She bought me the records I lusted for, the ones the rest of the family shouted at me tae turn doon!

But the simple chords I played on that red guitar began tae contrast wae an intricate counterpoint inside ma heid. I went up tae the big school struggling tae reconcile auld pals wae new pals, struggling wae nightmares, wae specs, plooks, my inability tae kick a ba'.

Velvet-collared jaickits and string ties that lingered in the wardrobe mocked me for lacking the confidence tae wear them. The energetic wee boay disappeared, in his place a right wee scunner – an impostor whose behaviour moved quickly fae mischief tae malevolence.

Katy could still coax a laugh out of me, but the comments of the ither two just demeaned me further. Eventually, inevitably, I took oan Faither, armed wae insults carefully crafted tae provoke a confrontation – and they did. The man had never so much as raised his voice tae any of his dochters but suddenly here he was – involuntarily lifting his haun tae his lunatic son. Ma mither squealed, but it was Katy who jumped between us before any blows landed. I'm the only one left tae recall that spectacle, but I remember the lessons it taught me.

By now, Katy had taken a different path fae the ither village lassies, finding an office job in the town and learning tae type at night school. She blossomed: shiny black and white photies bring these days sharply intae focus again: here's Katy in a ballroom somewhere, looking reet petite in polka-dots; there she is, all in black, leaning nonchalantly against a Sunbeam Rapier wae its 'Brylcreemed' driver. Aye – yoan Audrey Hepburn was jist a skinny version of oor Katy!

The ither two soon got married, Faither and I achieved a silent truce, and relative peace descended on our ménage – until a wee, square telly arrived. We would be watching, quite the thing, when Faither would suddenly roar at some Tory politician, sometimes even turnin' aff the set a'thegither and bringing oot the dominos. Daft! But this gave him the chance tae talk tae Katy. I pretended no tae listen, but marvelled tae massel as they discussed H-bombs in the Pacific, revolution in Cuba, satellites in space.

Faither was far fae daft; he cut his political teeth in the Ayrshire coalfields, and his dochter – who would turn up at the Young Socialists wearing a rather elegant turban – was weel up tae him. Wan night they talked about civil rights; I couldnae help massel, blurting oot something aboot black music and poverty in American ghettos. It felt as if somebody else was talking, but they heard me oot. On other nights, they would nurse me gently through the issues of the day – and I began tae think I might just have some ideas of ma ain, a voice of ma ain, and somebody who would listen.

Where dae they go, the years?

Ma studies took me tae Glesga, while Katy moved tae the Midlands wae 'Brylcreem Boy'. And stayed. For me, there were discoveries, disappointments, distractions – but Katy remained a constant, keeping me close. Postcards and bulky Christmas parcels found their way faithfully up the closes and through the doors of a long line of Glesga flats. Our two worlds became populated wae new people, we lost ithers, but these worlds were firmly aligned, often happily bumping thegither: we laughed as fights broke oot at family weddings, watched Live Aid thegither, got drunk in Brussels when she was on a demo (still her faither's dochter!).

I'm the one who's still here – not alone, but safe in the shelter of ma lifelong bond wae Katy – ma friend, teacher and lodestar: ma sister.

Kindness and Cakes

MARZIPAN FRUIT AND REAL MACAROONS

Marion Campbell

MY MUM AND MY aunt didn't talk for 16 years.

They lived in the same town and went to the same church. They had the same friends and went to the same Women's Guild.

Sixteen years.

The same coffee morning, pretending not to see.

Friends would speedily interrupt anyone about to make a clanging faux pas:

'Oh, May and Flora... they don't talk...'

It was never clear what the problem was, but it happened at the desperate time of the death of their mum, my gran. Grief sometimes misfires, and umbrage is taken. The object of the grief is no longer there to make anyone feel the need to make up again.

And then, it was all over.

I invited her to my wedding with my mother's consent – she accepted – she came – they talked – the cold war was over.

And then they were inseparable as before: phone calls at least twice every day, giggling walks with their dogs at the shore, getting their messages in Morrisons together, running each other to appointments... and sitting beside each other at the Guild.

The biggest difference to us as a family was suddenly we were inundated with pancakes and 'fancies'.

My aunt has the McLaren legs. Itchy varicose veins like sprawling rivers on a map, restless and bothersome. She finds sitting in front of the telly at night excruciating and her legs start to 'play up'.

I remember my gran, panthering about the living room in the evenings when she would come to stay. Restless legs.

Aunt May made use of her time.

Never to be caught idle, she would stand for hours and bake or make fancies. The baking was invariably pancakes or 'dropped scones' and the fancies were... an odd collection really: macaroons (the real potato ones) shaped into little hairy sausages; pale, minty peppermint creams, cut out with a bottle top and dipped in cooking chocolate (none of your Green and Black's); marzipan apples, pears and bananas, with a clove pushed in the top to look like that wee bit that joins it to the stem: walnuts with marzipan wrapped round them (a tiny hot-dog?); custard creams and fondant fancies. Nestling in decorative, paper cake holders, they were all unique and distinctive... and my mother loathed them.

My mum's tastes had changed so that she loved savoury things and couldn't abide sweet. Would never dream of ordering a pudding if we were out for a meal – always a starter. She couldn't be persuaded to eat even a slice of Terry's Chocolate Orange, and I'm sure she'd boak on a Creme Egg.

In the 16 years since they had spoken, her tastes had gone from sweet to sour and May had missed it.

As for letting May know about this? I suppose the rekindled friendship felt a little too new for that, a little too fragile. So she politely accepted the tokens of sisterly love with delight on her face and dread in her heart

So what to do with a gazillion fancies? I would have slid them off their plate and into the bin without a pang of conscience, but my mum was brought up during the war. She would keep a quarter slice of buttered bread in the breadbox... and eat it a couple of days later... even if it didn't taste nice... you can't reason with that kind of thinking.

Some Saturdays, my mum would travel up to Glasgow on the train. She liked Fraser's department store and Princes Square. Not for buying, just for looking, and sitting in a café enjoying the buzz of the city.

I always knew when she was going to go up because the night before she'd be in the kitchen for ages making packed lunches in bags like fury.

Ham sandwiches, cheese sandwiches, tuna, coronation chicken, whatever she had in the house. All on paper plates with ready buttered and jammed pancakes and half a dozen wee fancies, beautifully arranged with an accompanying bottle of water ('I wouldn't want them to wash it down with anything else!').

'They're someone's son or daughter Marion,' she would say, as I stifled an exasperated 'Muuuuuum...' She'd scuttle off with her 'bags'.

We'd be walking down Buchanan Street and she'd suddenly disappear from my side – mid-sentence sometimes. Sometimes I wouldn't notice and still be talking to her.

I felt an uneasy embarrassment.

I once asked her what their reactions were.

'Grateful, very polite, surprised and appreciative... never had anything else love.'

In my head though I can't help seeing a bewildered homeless person, sitting on the street, holding up a fondant cream and eyeing it suspiciously, maybe chucking it to his wee dog, who catches it first time with a resounding slap of its chops.

Or some street-hardened guy enduring a slagging from his friends, 'Check oot Malky wae the wee marzipan peach man!'

Worse still, what if my aunt came up to Glasgow, spotted one of her creations and recognised it? Would this mean another 16-year huff?

Not exactly legendary.

No-one in my family invented Blu-Tack, or discovered a spy, or survived a volcano – but a legendary huff? Legendary cakes? Legendary kindness?

FAITH, LOVE AND BANNOCKS

Beth Fullerton

'AYE, SHE COULD fairly mak bannocks!'

I've heard that expression many a time about my maternal grand-mother. If word got out that she was baking, my older brothers and cousins would all head off to her house and wait in anticipation at the back door, looking, as my grandfather put it, 'Like scorries aroond a herring barrel!' They would sit on her coalbox, eating hot bannocks with the butter slithering down their chins. I often wonder if it was the butter rather than the bannocks that was tastiest – like the mince scene in *The Steamie* when the ladies discuss whether it's the mince or the tatties which makes the meal!

Granny left school at 14 and went to work in a Church of Scotland manse. She used to say that she was too short to reach the top of the table and had to stand on a stool when the minister's wife taught her to bake. Those baking lessons stood her in good stead. I remember telling an elderly lady I used to visit that I had given up Cookery at school in favour of Latin. 'And much good it's likely done your husband!' she retorted, which was probably what Granny would have said!

Bannocks played a big part in feeding her family. Meals were eked out with bannocks dipped in the broth from boiled lamb and onions or soup made on a sheep's head or neck. My uncles' friends used to tell me 'We got many a hot bannock and butter from your grandmother and glad we were of it too!' It was the hungry '30s, yet Granny always had enough to go around and no-one seems to have been refused. If a baking was underway, all were welcome.

Granny's days were spent in an endless rota of housework. She had to fetch water from the communal pump in order to do dishes and laundry (all by hand), cleaning, mending, then in the evenings knitting goods to barter for groceries, intercepted by cooking three meals a day for her husband and family. All this was done in the two rooms that she, my grandfather and their nine children lived in. No wonder my mother often came home from school to find Granny crying – probably from the frustration that she had to do it all again the following day, and the constant worry of making ends meet.

Despite this she always managed to be kind and generous to any-one she thought was in need. 'She would have given her last,' they often said about her.

Yet that wasn't true about the youngest child she lost to scarlet fever in 1933. His passing had a severe effect on Granny. She blamed herself for insisting he go into hospital and thought maybe he would have survived had she kept him at home. Granny put away what few toys there were, and refused to talk about him. No flowers were to be put on his grave.

'If you can't do anything for the living, no point doing things after they are dead,' she would mutter, proclaiming too, 'I looked after him while he was alive, the Lord is looking after him now!' And that was it, for all the good it did my mother and her siblings whenever they spoke about him. To store away all his toys, yet not fully under-stand where their younger brother was, must have been very upsetting. For Granny however, it was the only way she could cope.

During the war years the family home was requisitioned by the army and they were given a brand new council house. When a gun post was positioned on the nearest street corner, Granny went out with many cups of tea and bannocks to the soldiers, loving to chat to them. A roaring fire was kept going to heat water so they could have baths. Word soon got around and they brought their friends along too! Along with soap and towels, she would provide them with the books which her own children had been given as prizes at school and church as gifts for their families. When one of my uncles came home on leave and complained about her being over-generous she snorted in reply, 'I'd like to think some woman would do the same for you!'

Perhaps it was as a reward for this that her three sons who saw active service returned home safely. Granny had the faith that God, having taken one son from her, surely wouldn't take another.

I never got to sample those famous bannocks. By the time I came along, the sixth child of her youngest surviving child, she was in her 70s and crippled with arthritis. Visiting her in the evenings, when she was upstairs in her bed, reminded me of the granny out of *Little Red Riding Hood*. Her hair was plaited and pinned around her head, a shawl around her shoulders and little round glasses on the point of her nose. Diabetes was claiming her eyesight and she would peer over those glasses and ask if I had learned to knit, grunting disapprovingly when Mam told her I was still too young. Perhaps, if joint replacements were available in the '60s, might have seen her in a different light.

There was also her final legacy to me – her insistence that the eldest daughter in each family be named Elizabeth after her. When she died and her birth certificate was found, the name on it was the shortened version, Betsy.

But what's in a name, when love was the essential ingredient in each and every one of her bannocks?

A CHRISTMAS GIFT

Martin Stepek

6 DECEMBER 1941. Somewhere in Siberia. It's cold, dark and the snow is feet thick.

On a cattle truck, stuck in a railway siding, hundreds of exhausted Poles are crammed, hungry and ill. They have recently been freed from the dreaded Siberian labour camps in the Arctic Circle, near Archangel, and are seeking to flee the Soviet Union, but they have few resources, and their energy is spent.

Four of the refugees are dear to me. My father is one. He is 19 years old. His two sisters, Zosia and Danka, are 16 and 14 and their mother Janina is 39. She has been unable to get up for two months now, desperately sick, worn out and starving. The family haven't eaten for a week, and are surviving by melting the snow on the ground and the icicles that form all day long on their cattle train.

Then another train, filled with Russians fleeing the advancing German forces, stops on the next track. All of the Polish refugees, aching with hunger, start to beg from the Russian people on the other train, and the Russians generously share some of their food with them.

Little Danka is watching this from the opened grille which serves as the carriage window. Jan and Zosia have been out begging, leaving her to tend to her mother. They return empty handed and are desolate.

Danka hears the word 'Divotchka' amongst the bustle of Polish beggars and Russian givers. Again she hears it – 'Divotchka'. It means little girl. She starts looking for the source. A Russian woman, wrapped in a thick fur coat and hat, is standing at the door of the other train. Danka stares at her. The woman is young and beautiful, maybe 30 years old. She stares back and smiles at the girl. Then she delves into the bag at her side and she throws something large and heavy straight at Danka. Instinctively Danka ducks but catches it. It is a huge loaf of bread. She looks up to thank the lady but she is gone.

This loaf feeds the family for a week. Without it they would all have died of hunger.

The date, 6th of December, is St Nicholas's Day. It is the day Polish children receive their Christmas presents.

I can never know who this woman was who saved my father and his two sisters and prolonged the life of my grandmother so that when she finally died of hunger in Teheran, she did so knowing that her children were free from the Soviet Union. Several other strangers, many of them impoverished peasants in Uzbekistan, Kazakhstan and Persia, shared what little they had to help my father and his family. And later, in 1946 when my father settled in Scotland, orphaned, his home destroyed, and his country Poland occupied by Stalin's Red Army, the Scottish people in turn treated him with friendship and kindness. It is due to the altruism of these complete strangers that I came to have a life, and in turn now have my own two Scottish children. My nine brothers and sisters and our children all owe our lives to these unknown people. Of all human traits it is this, human kindness in the most trying of times, which I think is most astonishing and moving, and it is our greatest source of hope.

The Folks at Home

NICE TRY, DAD!

Peter Laidlaw

'400 WORDS' IT SAID. 'Write 400 words about what you expect from university life and the best entry gets a crate of Stella Artois and the chance to write a Fresher's Diary for *Hype* magazine.' My father don't like Stella but pretending to be 19 instead of 69, and doing it in print, well he just couldn't resist that. So he wrote a short dialogue piece in the voices of various imaginary characters, the school chum, the girlfriend, a favourite teacher, his mother, etcetera, finishing off with some waffle about nervousness and self-doubt in what he hoped was a modest, 19-year-old, sort of way. If it won he meant to confess his little deception and demit the prize to the runner-up. But when it did win, the chance to prolong his fantasy life as a teenager in the pages of a student rag was just too much for him. If he could, even for a short time, persuade students that he was a contemporary, that would prove something, wouldn't it? So when Alex, the *Hype* editor, phoned with the good news and asked when Dad was going to collect the booze, he heard himself explaining that he'd prefer cash – to meet a bicycle tyre emergency – and could the money please be sent. (Dad was rather pleased with the 'youthful' telephone voice he'd used but Mum was deeply scornful.)

For the next week Dad plunged into all the Fresher's activities he could fit in during the day; and in the evenings filed his breathless copy in time for the next deadline. Shedding 50 years in print invigorated him, with the added frisson that it had to be reasonably convincing. So he found himself writing about pop bands, and the quality of the uni food, criticising a play at the Bedlam Theatre, attending a poetry reading at the Debating Club and an organ recital in St Giles'. All incognito of course. By day he was an inconspicuous old geri complete with hearing-aid and pebble specs; but at night... at night... In the glow of his computer monitor he was transformed. A virile, energetic youth bursting to enlighten his adoring public with his vivid prose, sparkling wit and oracular insight. But, and this was rather a chilling thought, aside from the actual wording, for proper verisimilitude he would have to tackle the tricky business of changing the prose natural to an old age pensioner to that of a teenager, and that is not easy. So he popped in the odd adjective, noun here and there, even a creative cliché or two, and he used the word 'got' a lot. He was fairly certain that his readers wouldn't spot his deception but Alex was quite another matter. Alex was an aspiring editor, already a graduate and clearly no fool. If Dad got his copy past him he'd won. So Alex became the actual target of my Dad's vanity and also, as it turned out, his nemesis.

Avoiding meeting Alex had not been difficult, all contact had been by email, and he'd only phoned Alex once. But shortly after the term started Dad got an invitation to a writers' meeting at the Students' Union. Going to it would have blown his cover – but there was a personal PS – apparently Alex couldn't be there and would Dad stand in for him to talk about writer recruitment or something. It would have been churlish to refuse.

On the day, and halfway into Dad's little spiel, in walked Alex instantly recognisable from his by-line picture. As he sat down in the front row there was an ominous smile of triumphal glee on his face.

When the meeting finished and as Dad went over to shake hands Alex was still smiling.

'Good to meet you Alex.'

'And you Mister Laidlaw, you write quite well for a fresher...'

'Perhaps not well enough; you knew didn't you?'

'Let's say I suspected...'

Dad's next question hung in the air for a moment as they looked at each other levelly.

'Something I wrote?'

'No.'

'What, then?'

Alex sighed, shifted his gaze and made to leave.

'It was the "puncture repair OUTFIT", the one you needed the money for, remember? Haven't heard it called that since my granny died.'

HAPPY HOLIDAYS

Mark Stephen

I ONCE OPENED the door of my parents' house to find my mum and dad newly returned from a caravanning trip. They had only been gone for three days and they'd driven less than 20 miles to Alford and yet they looked like they'd been in World War III. Dad was limping and had a big bandage round his head and Mum had her right arm in a triangular sling. Their car obviously hadn't been in a smash so, for the life of me, I couldn't work out how they'd managed to crock themselves so badly.

It went like this.

They had arrived at the caravan park, unhitched and set about pushing their elderly caravan into position. Mum slipped on wet grass and managed to stick her arm through the caravan window, gashing it rather badly. Now, my father loves a crisis, so he immediately took control. He sat Mum down in the caravan, wrapped a tea-towel about her arm, then set off at a run to phone for an ambulance (this was in the days before mobile phones).

Regulars at Haughton House Caravan Park will know it is as flat as a billiard table and almost entirely covered in soft, non-threatening grass, however, in the midst of 15 acres of sward lies one fist-sized rock. With unerring accuracy Dad sprinted towards it, tripped over it and sprained his ankle. He then hopped to the phone, called for help and hopped back to the caravan where poor Mum was not a happy bunny. She was still bleeding profusely and said that she was feeling sick. Dad diagnosed that this may have had something to do with the fact that the caravan was still rocking on its single axle due to the fact that he hadn't had time to jack it up yet.

He grabbed the handle and proceeded to jack up the caravan with the reckless speed which only an over-excited Technical teacher is capable of in these situations. In fact he cranked the handle so violently that the end of it slipped off the bolt, flew up and cracked him squarely between the eyes, splitting his forehead and rendering him temporarily insensible.

By the time the First Aid Team arrived they were met with two casualties, not the one they had expected and the caravan looked like it had been decorated by Quentin Tarantino.

Even by my parents' standards (and they are about as accident-prone as the Chuckle Brothers), this was a remarkable tale. As soon as they had finished explaining I said to them, 'So, did you have a nice time then?'

'Oh yes, lovely,' they beamed. 'It's just nice to get away.'

Bless.

War Stories

RONALD GOLD RN

1914–1986

Jacqui Adams

A TELEGRAM WAS BAD NEWS. Everybody knew that, so when one arrived at the tenement house that the Gold family had been allocated to, Nanny Gold began wailing and screeching. My Aunty Joy tore it open, cheered and said, 'Stop it Mum. Ron's safe. We have to go to Victoria for him today.'

Three days before a telegram had arrived to say that Ronald Gold was missing at sea. His ship had been torpedoed and had sunk. No-one knew who was safe.

Grandad and Aunty Joy left straightaway to meet Uncle Ron at Victoria Railway Station without knowing if he was injured. He had been sent home with no idea that the house had been bombed or where the family had moved to.

The station was packed with people, some in civvies, some in uniform and it was very noisy. The smell of burning coals, steam blowing and the whistles from the train made Aunty Joy excited and she started hopping on both legs alternatively till Grandad threatened to wallop her. A guard holding a clipboard was walking around the people waiting.

Joy pulled the guard's sleeve and shouted above the noise.

'Is Ronald Gold on your list? He's a signalman and his ship got torpedoed days ago.'

'Slow down. Who?'

'RONALD GOLD. HE'S MY BROTHER AND HE'S...'

'Calm down. Calm down. Yes, he's here.'

'Where?'

'On my list. The train won't be in for a while so go and sit quietly.'

Pop disappeared into the bar and left Joy to sit swinging her feet. She started trying to count the rivets on the steel arches in the station but somebody tapped her shoulder and made her jump.

'What are you doing here?' a voice said.

Joy's brother Donald was standing next to her. Joy explained about Ron and told him that the house they lived in had been bombed. Donald dropped his kit bag at Joy's feet and said he'd go and find Pop.

'Easy peasy. He's in the bar and mum won't half give him what for if he goes home drunk!'

Just as Don got to the bar there was a whistle from a train in the distance. Everybody rushed to the gates but the guards blocked them off. With a lot of hissing and clouds of steam the train pulled in, windows were pulled down, hands reached out and turned the door handles. Men poured out and started walking down the platform.

'I can see Ron,' Joy said, then she burst out laughing.

'He looks so funny in his vest and pants!'

Grandad gave her a clout round the ear and she burst into tears. Ron walked up to them. True enough, he was only in a tatty vest and pants and his feet were bare!

Ron was shivering and his teeth chattered as he said, 'We lost everything when the ship went down and the ship that rescued us did their best but they had to give the injured men blankets and there wasn't enough to go round.'

Don got his pyjamas and socks from his kit bag and helped a shivering Ron put them on. Aunty Joy offered Ron her socks but she had tiny feet so Grandad gave him his. They headed for home.

When they got on to the trolleybus the conductor wouldn't take any money for the ride as he saw the state that Ron was in. Joy whispered to Don, 'Just as well as Dad drank most of the money in the station!'

As they got off the trolleybus, walked slowly and quietly past some of the bombed buildings, Ron asked Joy why she was still in London.

Joy was quiet for a minute, then she replied, 'Mum brought me back from the people I was evacuated to as they were cruel and made me ill. I got taken to hospital.'

Sixty-five years later she told me, her niece, the full story and it brought tears to my eyes.

The next day Ron wrote a letter to the *Sunday Express* newspaper. In it he said he was disgusted at the way the sailors from his ship had been treated. Winston Churchill wanted every man to do his duty but surely the British Empire could have at least provided blankets for the rescued sailors. After all, if they all caught pneumonia they wouldn't be fighting for the country, would they? To the family's surprise the letter was printed in the very next *Sunday Express* and everybody cheered Ron when he popped down the pub before lunch. Two days later Ron received a letter from somebody 'high up' saying they were very sorry that Signalman Ronald Gold had been unhappy about his treatment on rescue. It also thanked him for his part in keeping the country safe. My nanny was very proud as all her 'boys' hadn't had a lot of education. She hid the copy of the newspaper under her mattress. Two weeks later Ron went back to sea but he always slept with a blanket under his pillow just in case.

PRISONER!

Nuala Abramson

THE AIR IN THE cabin was tense. We were not talking much so the crackling voice of the pilot in the cockpit was easily heard, even over the droning engine.

'Going over now boys, ready to jump?'

The door was pushed open roughly, letting a roaring blast of air in, freezing us through our layers of padding. I realised this was the most terrifying thing I had ever done in my life. Launching through the air with only a bit of silk to keep me up, if I was captured I wouldn't last long with my Jewish surname, even if I didn't practice Judaism. However with the captain barking at me I didn't have time to make myself even more terrified. After a last look at my comrades I closed my eyes and plummeted into the limitless air.

It was madness really, to think we could last a second in enemy territory. They picked us up, or shot us down, as soon as we came near the ground. They bundled us into rattling vans, shouted orders in hard German and expected us to stand for the three hours it took to get to the prisoner of war camp. We were sore and exhausted by the time we arrived and we could hardly march to our cold wooden cabins. After some more orders and insults I crashed into my hard bed and went straight into an uneasy sleep.

When I woke up to the harsh barks of the Nazi captains I thought I was back in my training days. Then I realised. I was a prisoner! What would my mother think? How would my sisters react? Would my brother, Will, be informed? He was also in a POW camp, surely the Nazis, however brutal, would let him know? All these questions were racing around in my mind so fast I did not notice a huge German guard march up to me until he shouted that I was to attend a 'session of questions' in ten minutes. I quickly got myself moving down to where he had shown me on the unclear map and walked cautiously into the dark, timbered building.

Over the next couple of weeks I forgot that first session of questions. It was eclipsed by the hard work I had to do. We were treated according to the Geneva Convention but we were obviously despised by the Nazis. If it wasn't for my new friends I would have been permanently gloomy. The worst day though was a calm Sunday when we were allowed to rest for a while as we liked. At about 11 o'clock, Private John was quietly asked by a limping sergeant to go with him. No-one knew what this was about but John managed a weak smile then left us. He never returned. After that day we were wary of any soldier coming stamping into our hut so when the same limping sergeant stepped into the door all our hearts sank. The man looked round with his expressionless blue eyes until he found me.

'Private Ernest?' he questioned. 'You are to step this way.'

I was terrified but tried not to show it as I said goodbye to my friends. I knew they were thinking the same thing as me. I was another Private John. The soldier marched me to a van then ordered me in. The whole bumpy journey was taken up by horrible thoughts of firing squads, the rumoured 'death camps' and my family weeping over the letter stating my death. Finally we arrived at a large camp, rounded by barbed wire. It was like the one I had been in before but it somehow had a slightly happier aura about it. Whatever it was, it wasn't a 'death camp'.

The silent driver escorted me to a small square hut. He left me inside its only room and gestured to me to sit on the only chair. I was getting bored and stiff on its hard surface when I heard people opening the door and walking down the small hall. Immediately I recognised one of the voices, one of the laughs, one of the smiles! It was my beloved big brother Will! I had never known how much I had missed him until that moment. I didn't know why he was with me but one thing was certain. Work would never be hard again.

This is a true story about my great, great uncles, Will and Ernie, seen through Ernie's eyes. They were both paratroopers captured during World War II. I have stuck to the facts as closely as I could but their story was not considered very important so there are no records save for what my mother's side of the family know. I was inspired to write it by the question of why people, who could brutally kill over six million Jews, could put two brothers, one an officer and one a private, into the same prisoner of war camp.

My family and I still do not know, but perhaps, as Anne Frank said, 'People are really good at heart.'

TOUGH LUCK

Marita Lück

SHE IS A TOUGH COOKIE, my Tante Leni, despite her delicate and styled appearance. Slender and dignified, always immaculately dressed, immaculately coiffed, head held high, getting up two hours earlier than anyone else, to put on her make-up and do her hair, to get ready to face the world.

After the war, she trained as a nurse, married a Scottish psychiatrist, moved to England, changed her name from Helene to Helen. For me, she will always be Tante Leni.

In the 1970s, she divorced her cheating husband, left him and their two adult sons, and moved back to Germany. Being an expert in cosmetics and fragrance, she found employment with a perfumery in Hamburg, and could afford a small flat of her own. In her late 40s, she married again.

Leo Lück, one of her second cousins, had emigrated to America soon after the war. He owned 'Luck Garages' in Ohio, his skills as a mechanic, combined with his lucky surname, made him a rich man. Unfortunately, Helen found out a little too late that he was an alcoholic. Not one to suffer foolish husbands gladly, she divorced Leo after a couple of years, but stayed in America, working as a nurse.

Not an ordinary nurse, though. Helen Lück, now approaching her 60s, still fragrant and a pleasure to behold, looked after wealthy pensioners. A private nurse. She fell in love with one of her elderly protégées, Al, a retired US Marine, and he fell in love with her. Al and Tante Leni married and lived happily – almost ever after – for 18 years. After his death, she sold their holiday home in Florida and now enjoys life in her own flat in Ohio. She still drives her own car and soon, she will celebrate her 83rd birthday.

Born in 1928 in Radomsko in the South of Poland to a German family, she grew up with her brother Richard and her sister Lucy. In January 1945, 16-year-old Helene took a train to visit a friend but she never returned to the family home. The Russian army had invaded and turned Poland into a war zone, her train back home ran into the thick of the fighting. Scared to death, Helene jumped out of the train, and together with hundreds of soldiers, she found another train that took her to the north of Poland. There she hoped to take shelter in her uncle's – my grandfather's – farm. But the farm was deserted. All German families had left just two hours earlier, with their horses and carts, to join the refugee trek to the West. They were gone. Just two hours earlier!

Helene walks the empty trail through the snow, desperate to catch up. In front of her, only empty tracks and hoof prints. She gives up. Then she hears a freight train. It doesn't have a roof. In the chaos and the cold, she holds on to her travel bag she had packed only for her trip to visit a friend, and jumps on the train. It goes west, and that's where she hopes to find her family.

'If we ever become separated,' her father had told her, 'try to reach our friends' farm near Hanover.' Hanover. 400 miles west.

Finally, Helene's train reaches Dresden in East Germany. She decides to take a rest. The city is full of refugees, the population increased to 1.2 million, twice as many as Dresden's residents. It is thought to be safe from air raids, as there is no significant military, or industry. Helene finds shelter in a former school, a five-storey building. Every day, she goes to the train station, helps by looking after other refugees who are put up in the station.

On 13 February 1945, Helene receives a warning from a friend: 'Don't go to the station today. There will be a massive air raid.' Helene hides in the cellar of the school, along with 300 others. Minutes later, the first bombs turn the building into rubble. Helene doesn't remember how she escaped from the cellar. But to this day, Helen remembers in her dreams. Bad dreams. Flames everywhere. Buildings collapsing, people running, screaming, dying. Helene, coat over her head, spends the night in a park.

In the morning, Dresden is full of burned corpses, many shrunk to a quarter of their size. 1,500 degrees centigrade in the blast, they say, at least 25,000 dead, 15 square miles turned to ashes. To this day, all church bells ring on 13 February in Dresden. But young Helene doesn't know this as yet. Only Helen will know, much much later.

Helene doesn't know how she lost her sturdy leather shoes. Only her socks protect her from the snow as she walks out of the city. There is no food – sometimes she eats turnips she finds on deserted fields. Helene walks over 200 miles to Hanover. The Allies stop her, suspect her of being a spy. She just says 'I am looking for my parents.' Her plight moves them, they give her food, chocolate – and better still: travel papers. She keeps walking until, in June 1945, six months after her odyssey began, she reaches the farm near Hanover her father had mentioned. But her family isn't there, nobody knows their fate. Helene stays on the farm until October 1945, when, out of the blue, her mother arrives to collect her. She had taken the first bus that had become available from Hanover, to look for her daughter, not knowing whether she would find her on that farm, or not. Thus, Helene was reunited with all her family – her mother, father, sister, and later also her brother.

You know the rest...

In 2003, when America prepared for war, Helen spoke to an American newspaper. 'If there would be another war, I would probably survive again, as long as there is a reason to survive,' she said, aged 74. That's my Tante Leni. Or Helene Lück. Slender and dignified, always immaculately dressed, immaculately coiffed, head held high, getting up two hours earlier than anyone else, to put on her make-up and do her hair, to get ready to face the world.

HE WASN'T A LEGEND

Stephen Bullock

HE WASN'T A LEGEND, but his stories were legendary. My Grandad Fred nearly died, met Winston Churchill, was promoted, demoted, beachheaded in Italy and on D-Day, felt the heat of explosions, and captured a company of German soldiers. Almost. But these were not tales of gun-toting derring-do. Grandad Fred's war was humorous and human, and from the tales he chose to tell, he probably never loaded his gun.

Somewhere in Europe a convoy was crossing a pontoon, a temporary bridge, and Grandad Fred's jeep was queuing in the heat. Shirts off, the three of them sunbathed against the tyres and nodded off. Grandad Fred was woken by someone shaking his shoulder.

Grandad Fred looked around. The pontoon was gone. The entire battalion was gone. It was a four-hour drive to the nearest bridge, and another four to catch up with the battalion. A poetic justice and practical joke sandwich for lazy privates sleeping on the job.

'Where is your commanding officer?'

Grandad Fred looked up and realized his waker was a soldier. A German soldier.

Fear and silence. Their rifles were in the jeep. They weren't even loaded.

'Your battalion is nearby, yes? There are only a hundred of us. We wish to surrender.'

'Surrender?'

'Yes.'

'To us?'

'Yes.'

'A hundred of you?'

'Yes.'

Horror and silence.

'They're just over that hill. You can surrender there. You can't miss them.'

'Danke.' He saluted, they saluted back, and off he marched.

Still shirtless they jolted and skidded away and didn't dare to look back.

Having almost captured a company of Germans Grandad Fred

enjoyed the thrill of promotion. Lance Corporal. His first task wa
the night watch at camp, including responsibility for an Italia
prisoner the officers had nicknamed Houdini. Houdini was predic
tably gone by morning and a frenzied search discovered he ha
tunnelled out of his cell with a spoon, only to surface into th
building next door. He was apprehended eating breakfast in th
Officers' Mess and Grandad Fred's stripes lasted less than a day.

As a communications operator Grandad Fred spent a fe
months in the trenches looking after the telephone that linked the
to the rest of the battalion. For weeks they huddled in the dark
learning to ignore the shells that landed nearby. After weeks o
listless nothingness the order to go 'over the top' was imminent an
the whole trench was electrified, waiting.

The three of them that slept beside the telephone were tucke
up in their bunks when a shell blew the side of the trench in. On
of the privates was buried alive where he slept. To dig him ou
before he suffocated was a desperate and muddy affair. A singl
shovel, tin mugs, their hands. Heap after heap of soil and ston
was abandoned behind them as they fought for their friend. The
dragged him, black and half-conscious, from his muddy tomb
Catching their breaths, with relieved white grins, they heard
strange noise coming from the pile of earth they had moved of
their comrade. A muffled clacking. A ringing almost. They ha
buried the telephone.

By the time they dug it out the ringing had stopped, th
battalion had engaged the enemy, and Fred's platoon had misse
the party.

In this way Grandad Fred casually avoided the bloodiness o
battle, despite being at the centre of the conflict. His platoon wer
hitching a ride with a vessel so crumpled by the enemy, trans
porting battle-bandaged soldiers so poorly weaponed and exhauste
that as they landed upon a heavily defended beach the Italia
artillery took pity and ceased fire. Grandad Fred and the other troop
hobbled calmly across the silent, burnt beach to the protection o
the dunes before the screaming shell bombardment began again.

I remember asking Grandad Fred why he started smoking, an
he always told me that it was because it saved his life. His jeep wa
leading a long convoy along a long, boring road, and the rest of th
jeep implored Fred to pull over and stop for a cigarette. Fred didn'

smoke, never had, but for some reason he stepped out of character and pulled the jeep over. They shared around the smokes and lit up their 'lucifers' as the rest of the convoy caught up. The first armoured vehicle sailed past, continued for a few metres and blew up into the air. The force from the landmine rolled it over, casting aside pieces of its guts and everyone inside was killed instantly.

Fred was even there at D-Day. The intelligence they were working from was wrong and their small boat ruddered by a 16-year-old American soldier was headed into a heavily protected and mined part of the beaches. The young American had been squinting at the shore for some time, deafened by exploding shells and crashing waves. 'Does anyone here know Morse?' he finally hollered. The fresh-faced yankee had not even completed his basic training. The complex flashes bouncing off a handheld mirror on the shore were meaningless to him, but as a communications operator it was like reading a book for Grandad Fred. He quickly interpreted the danger and they landed far further along the coast. An unimpressive, life-saving moment.

I promised Winston Churchill. Grandad Fred's platoon was meeting an air transport, a Halifax or something, it didn't matter to the tale. The commanding officers were eager to be the first to greet the visitors, straightening their uniforms as Churchill himself ambled awkwardly down the stepladder. The officers were made to wait. Toilet breaks aren't written into the history books but they happened. After several hours in a vibrating aircraft the task fell to Private Fred to personally stand guard as Winston Churchill un-buttoned and relieved himself behind the nearest tree. Job done, he wiped a damp hand on his trousers and patted Fred on the shoulder. 'I needed that,' he said.

MY FAMILY STORY

Olivia Webster

DURING A BOMBING raid by the Germans in World War II in Old Aberdeen my great, great auntie had a lucky escape! An air raid siren went off when she was in her bed but sadly she was deaf and did not hear it! She luckily got up for a cup of tea. While she was waiting for the kettle to boil there was some drama going on outside that she wasn't aware of. When she arrived back in her bedroom with her cup of tea she found somthing very unusual in her bed. While she had been in the kitchen getting a cup of tea a bomb had dropped outside the church next door. The bomb had landed in the graveyard and the blast had sent one of the gravestones high into the air and straight through my great, great auntie's roof. As she looked in horror at the massive gravestone lying exactly where she had been five minutes earlier, she was very glad she had felt the urge for a little cuppa!

FREEDOM AT LAST

Margaret MacPherson

IN THE SPRING of 1945 the villages of Glenelg and Arnisdale gave a welcoming home party for my father, Roderick MacPherson, after five years in a prisoner of war camp in Germany. He had been captured in May 1940 at Abbeville after Dunkirk with most of the others from his battalion of the Seaforth Highlanders.

They were marched into a field and lined up by the SS and a machine gun was wheeled in; before they had a chance to start firing, the regular German army arrived and they were ordered out of the field and on to the road for a long journey to their prison camp. They were put on a barge in France without food or water and then marched to the camp, Stalag 10C, which was in Bleicherode, near Nordhausen.

For about the first six months in the camp, before the Red Cross got through, he was posted as missing and his family back in Glenelg didn't know if he was dead or alive. However, his uncle in Glenelg sent him a letter anyway, addressed to: 'Roderick Mac-Pherson, Private 337, Prisoner of War, Germany', which he miraculously received.

He spent the first years working in a salt mine and then later on building sites and life was very hard but sometimes he came across acts of unexpected kindness. The German families were allowed to ask for a prisoner to do work for them on Sundays. This was usually the day off for prisoners. The families were often risking being shot if the prisoner escaped while in their care. A farmer had asked for my father to help him out on the farm and when my father arrived and asked what work he should get started on, he was told, 'You're to do nothing, sit at the table and have a proper meal.'

Later he showed my father a photograph of a boy in a German army uniform and told him it was their son who had been killed fighting in France. Then on a building site where he was working the German guard started leaving a couple of roll-up cigarettes on the wall near to where my father was working for him to find when it was time to go back to camp.

After four years in the camp he became seriously ill with a

stomach ulcer and spent six months lying on his back in a prisoner of war hospital. He was taken there by train, by two guards who seated themselves and my father in a civilian carriage. An old German woman in the carriage asked the soldiers what was wrong with him and she was told that the prisoner was very sick and they were taking him to hospital but there was no hope and he was going to die, which my father understood as over the years had picked up some of the German language. The old lady would look at him every now and again and start crying.

He was lucky that he was attended to in the hospital by a Harley Street doctor (a prisoner of war himself obviously) and did in fact recover. The whole time he was in hospital he sent letters home to his mother in Glenelg without ever telling her he was in hospital. Because he had been so ill he was repatriated a few months before the end of the war and when he arrived back in Scotland he visited all the homes of his fellow prisoners of war from the Highlands to give them news of their sons. He was never bitter and he never complained about his time in Germany and never let it affect his life. In fact he always said he regretted not having hitchhiked back to Germany after the end of the war to look for the German people who had been kind to him and to thank them.

Before the war he had worked on his mother's croft, his father had died when he was 15. His pride and joy was his motorbike that he carefully tied up and hung from the rafters in the barn when he left for the war. Throughout the whole five years his mother wouldn't let anybody touch or use the motorbike because it had to be there for him when he came home. When he arrived home he untied his motorbike, charged the battery and off he sped up and over Mam Ratagan, the high mountain road out of Glenelg. He was free, he was on his motorbike, and he was home.

The prize at the end of his five years in Germany was to meet my mother at his homecoming party, she had worked in service as a cook and was in Glenelg visiting her married sister and had been asked to bake the cake for his party. My father often joked that she took advantage of him not knowing what he was doing when he got back and that he was probably suffering from shell shock.

When he died aged 90 in 2009 the funeral was held in Glenelg and was a very beautiful and moving affair. The church was full and many were left standing outside. When his coffin was carried out of the church the men then took it in turns in groups of six to carry his coffin further up the village to the waiting hearse. They all wanted a chance to show their respect.

WHEN GRANNY WORKED IN MILLAR'S

Catriona Child

EVERYONE, OR I hope everyone, has one of those jobs. A job that bridges the gap between being a teenager and being a grown-up. A job that, even though you might not realise it at the time, you look back on with affection and nostalgia. Millar's was that job for Granny. William Millar and Son's Grocer's Shop in Dundee. Granny was a legend to us but she also made legends of the people who were lucky enough to share her life.

On the 70th anniversary of Dunkirk last year, I sat with my mum and we both cried for a man we'd never met. A man who'd died before either of us were born, but a man we felt we knew because of Granny's stories of her time at Millar's.

It all stared when Granny was 14 and her mother saw a job in the paper. Millar's the grocers were looking for staff. There were no job applications in those days; Granny was sent off that morning to enquire about the position. According to Granny, the interview went something like this:

Mr Millar: So, Susan, you're here about the job?

Granny: My name's not Susan, it's Geraldine.

Mr Millar: I know that, but I'm going to call you Susan. Congratulations, you've got the job. Let's get you started.

Granny: But, what about school? My mum will wonder where I am.

Mr Millar: No more school for you, Susan.

Granny was led onto the shop floor, where Mr Millar gave her an apron to wear and left her standing behind a till. The apron was far too big for her and trailed under her feet. Granny was in tears now, no idea what she was supposed to be doing and with everyone staring at her: the 'new girl'.

Enter her knight in shining armour: Willie Boyle.

He introduced himself, and got her to stand on a chair while he pinned the hem of her apron up. He then showed her how to work the till, and told her that if anyone gave her any bother she was to let him know.

Granny was smitten.

When World War II broke out, Willie, along with all the other boys in the shop, left for the army. Willie died at Dunkirk. One of the other boys brought the news. He'd found Willie lying in a ditch at the side of the road. He'd stopped to help him, but after speaking to him for a few minutes, he knew Willie wasn't coming home. Willie's mother used to come into the shop and speak to Granny about him. His mother never believed he was dead, always believed he'd come home some day. Granny knew the truth, but never said anything. She would always cry when she told us this story. She'd show us his letters and the one photo she had of him. Handsome in his uniform. She'd kept them safe all these years. Little did Willie know when he made the decision to rescue Granny and pin up the hem of her apron, that years later her daughter and granddaughter would remember him on the anniversary of his death.

Willie was Granny's favourite but there were others she told us about. Two names in particular stand out: Philip Lindsay and George Auchterlonie. They both died in the desert. George's wife was pregnant when he died, and he must have known he wasn't going to make it back as he wrote a letter to his unborn daughter. One of the ladies in the shop took the letter to D.C. Thomson's, and they traced over it with newspaper ink, so the pencil wouldn't fade before his daughter was old enough to read it. Years later, George's daughter turned up asking to hear stories about the father she never got to meet.

Out of all the boys who worked in the shop, only two survived the war: William Millar's sons. Granny would shake her head at the irony of Dunkirk. While Willie was dying at the side of the road, the Millar boys were staging their own slapstick comedy routine. On the beaches of France, with thousands of British troops desperately trying to avoid the gunfire and make it home, somehow they managed to find a boat.

'You'd think one of them would have wondered why it was just sitting there, ignored by everyone else,' Granny used to say.

In they climbed, and started rowing out to sea. They got a few metres before they realised that water was starting to come in from a hole in the bottom of the boat. They frantically tried to get back to shore, but ended up having to wade most of the way back to the beach after the boat sank underneath them.

The war separated people, but it also brought them together.

One night Granny went to stay with Cath, one of the other girls who worked in Millar's. During the night there was an air raid, and Cath's older brother came in to make sure they were okay. Granny was horrified, and would always mimic the action of pulling the blankets right up to her chin. Not only had Cath never mentioned any brother, but to have such a handsome one too. For him to have seen her in bed with her rollers in was too much to bear. Cath's brother obviously didn't mind though, as he later became Granddad.

Granny always said she could write a book about her time at Millar's, but she never got round to it. Maybe one day, I'll attempt to write it for her. For now I hope that this is enough to allow Granny and the people she cared about to maintain their legendary status.

A FINE SOJER LADDIE

Fran Brady

June 1916

RECRUITING SERGEANT MACFARLANE was having a poor morning. The heady days of '14 and '15 were over. The wave of patriotism that had swept the country was ebbing fast and the sheen of a glorious adventure in a foreign land was dulled by the lists of casualties and stories of life in the trenches. The country was running out of young men fit enough to pass the army medical even though the bar had been lowered. This morning, only three out of half a dozen new volunteers had passed.

Then Robert Brady walked in. Tall, broad-shouldered, well-muscled and with a spark in his eyes that reminded Macfarlane of the early days, when high adventure – or at least escape from poverty and tedium – had been anticipated. The lad sailed through the medical, filled out the forms and was issued with the Black Watch uniform.

And a fine laddie he looked in it! Enough to inspire fear into the Huns. Young, of course, probably not the 17 he had written on his form, but hopefully at least the minimum age of 16. Macfarlane did not ask any questions. He was not about to turn down the best offer he had had all morning.

Robert had money in his pocket, a rare experience for him. He had gone without fags for several days to save up the price of the ferry ticket but the ferryman had waved his money away when Robert had told him he was going to Dundee to join up. A shop across the road from the recruiting office advertised 'Fine Pictures of Soldiers in Uniform – Developed While You Wait'.

The idea that he was already a soldier was irresistible. Half an hour later, he was outside the shop, proudly clutching the photo.

Six months ago, he had started 'doon the pit'. Every boy in Buckhaven looked forward to the day he became a real man among men in the dirt and the danger.

But he hadn't bargained for the darkness. It oppressed him more each day though he tried to ignore it. His father, Terry Brady, was a legend in the pit. It was unthinkable that his laddie would be 'a feirdiegowk'.

He knew that he had to find a way out. The army recruitment poster caught his eye, Kitchener's finger pointing straight at him. His country needed him. And he needed to get out of his country. He would join up and go to the war in France.

How to get away from the pit and over the River Tay to Dundee to the recruitment office, the address of which was written along the bottom of the poster, was the problem. Then Father took to his bed with one of his chest infections, running a fever as he lay in the bed in the recess, coughing black spit into rags that Mother threw on the fire.

Robert had set off alone for the pit but with no intentions of reaching it. Instead he had crept home and stealthily wheeled his father's bike out. His legs were aching with the effort to reach the pedals.

His mother burst into tears when he swaggered into the miners' row cottage.

'Ye'll be killed, son. They're a' coming back deid,' she sobbed.

'Dinnae greet, Maw. Ah'm goan' tae be a fine sojer laddie. Are ye no' prood? Do Ah no' look jist braw?' He twirled, making the heavy kilt swing out and the big sporran bounce.

The next minute he was on the floor, his head spinning with the blow.

'Ye young fool! Whit dae ye think ye're playin' at?' roared his father. He had leapt out of bed and now he towered over Robert, the breath rasping in his constricted chest. 'Tak' that get-up aff this meenit.'

Sergeant Macfarlane had an even worse morning the next day. Not only did half of the new volunteers prove unfit for active service but the fine young lad, yesterday's only bright spot, was marched into the office by an irate man with a grey face and a hacking cough.

'He's no' even 16 yet. He cannae join up. Ye're no' getting him for yer bloody cannon-fodder.'

And he flung the uniform on the desk and marched the lad out of the door before Macfarlane even had time to reply.

Footnote:

The Battle of the Somme, between July and November 1916, was one of the bloodiest military operations ever recorded. One and a half million young men died.

It would be another nine months before Robert went to war

and made his own discovery about just what a fine adventure it was not. There would be times in the trenches when he thought almost fondly of the pit.

But, thanks to his father, Terry, he missed the Somme and lived to pass the photograph on to his grandchildren.

SECRET HERO

Lyanne Mitchell

MY DAD WAS A BIG, quiet man. On one subject, he was especially quiet: what he did in World War II. My brother and I were teenagers before he felt we were mature enough to understand. One day, he decided to tell us. The family was sitting around the living-room table after Sunday lunch. Dad began to tell his story. He spoke in a quiet voice and I can still remember his discomfort. He was not good with words, he said.

As a boy, he had been deeply influenced by the Society of Friends, better known as the Quakers. He admired their involvement in social action and their commitment to peace. He was an idealistic young man. He used to attend 'Band of Hope' meetings.

'You always got a bun and a mug of tea at the end,' he said with a grin.

He loved belting out their signature hymn with its rousing repeating chorus:

'Trust in God – Trust in God – Trust in God and do the right.'

War came and Dad was conscripted into the army. He would not go into details, simply saying that he could not stomach losing his identity and blindly carrying out orders to fight and kill other young men who were equally caught up in the machinery of war. He decided to become a conscientious objector.

The army's response was swift. The 'conchies' were rounded up and stage one of corrective treatment began. Ridicule and humiliation. Small men were issued with large uniforms and huge helmets and boots. Big men were forced into too-small uniforms, helmets and boots. They were made to parade in front of their former fellow soldiers, who howled and jeered at them in derision. More than half of the small group gave up right there. From then on, the army's treatment became steadily more and more severe. Interrogation, beatings, starvation and solitary confinement. My dad was a butcher to trade. He was no stranger to blood and guts. He was no coward!

'At one point, we were taken out to an open field and tied down on the ground and left there, as German bombing raids flew overhead,' Dad said, almost in a whisper.

'We were left to die. But there was a Welsh Sergeant-Major who had compassion. He crawled out and released us, telling us to run for cover. I'll never forget that man.'

Dad refused to answer during interrogation and this was officially entered in army files as 'dumb insolence'. His only support was occasional visits made by local Quakers. He said that this is what kept him going through this darkest of times because he felt he was not completely alone in his beliefs. Finally, he was told that he would be taken out and shot at dawn if he would not capitulate. He spent one night believing that he would die in the morning.

Haltingly, almost in a whisper, he told us, 'I just held on to this simple belief – so long as there is one person in this world who refuses to fight and kill, there will be hope for humankind.'

Morning came, and of course, he was not shot. This had been the final attempt to break his will. He was transferred for trial and was sentenced to civic prison which Dad said was like a holiday camp compared to army prison. Eventually, he was released to serve out the rest of the war in the Land Army. He worked on a farm and delivered milk with a horse and cart. This is where he met my mother, who was the farm bookkeeper. He was 18. My mother said that she took him for a man in his 30s. Such was the physical impact of his experiences on his appearance.

My parents' courtship was not an easy one. My mother's brother, who was a pilot in the RAF, was declared 'missing in action' during the Battle of Britain, and eventually the family were notified that he had been shot down over France. My father was not welcomed in my mother's home and they had to meet well away from her family. Dad said that the stigma against 'conchies' never went away within his generation. He was aware of it all his life but he never regretted his decision.

My mother and father died in 1995. On Armistice Day, I always wear two poppies; a red poppy to honour my uncle and all servicemen who died in World War II and subsequent wars; and a white poppy, in honour of my brave father and other conscientious objectors, who stood up for their beliefs in the face of vicious physical and mental torture.

When I was asked for his favourite hymn for his funeral service, there was no hesitation in my choice. We sang:

'Courage, brother! do not stumble,
Though thy path is dark as night;
There's a star to guide the humble
Trust in God and do the right.

'Some will hate thee, some will love thee,
Some will flatter, some will slight;
Turn from man, and look above thee,
Trust in God and do the right.

'Simple rule and safest guiding,
Inward peace and inward light;
Star upon our path abiding,
Trust in God and do the right.'

Making Their Own History

LOOK STAR WALKER

Sergio Burns

STARS, THEY SAY, are held together by gravity. Football legends are held together by something less tangible, like the cosmic glue of sporting history. The Wayne Rooney of a different galaxy and time was a gentleman. He was my mother's uncle, her father's brother, who played for Heart of Midlothian, Chelsea and Scotland.

Born on 26 May 1915, Tommy Walker joined Hearts' ground staff early in 1932, but the Livingston-born über-player was too young to sign on and was farmed out to Linlithgow Rose until he was 17. Even at this tender age his potential was obvious and he was soon a regular in the 1933–4 Hearts side, a teenage prodigy thrilling Jambos with his soccer wizardry. Early ambitions to be a Church of Scotland minister were trampled under football boots that glided across the playing surface of Tynecastle Park, Edinburgh. Arsenal and Liverpool came calling for the talented footballer, with the former reportedly offering a then world (if not intergalactic) record, £12,000 for Walker's skills. A threatened rebellion of fans put paid to any thoughts of the club selling their teenage starlet and greatest asset, he remained at Heart of Midlothian.

Despite his brilliance, Walker never won a major piece of silverware in his Tynecastle playing career. A second place in the Scottish League in 1937–38, trailing Celtic by three points, was as close as he came to touching glory. He did, however, grace the Scottish international side with his presence on 21 occasions, a soccer genius in a time of few international call-ups. Today he would have commanded many appearances for his country and millions of euros, or even dollars, for his services. In the contemporary football universe he would have been offered a gigantic salary (an astronomic Rooney-esque £120,000 per week) to play in any of the world's top leagues.

I can imagine him being pulled, unceremoniously, into the rear of a limousine by Real Madrid's José Mourinho, Manchester United's Alex Ferguson or Barcelona's Josep 'Pep' Guardiola, a contract discussed concomitant with agreements over colossal fees for image rights and branding sponsorship.

I can imagine them saying:

'Whatever you want....want...want...want...want.'

In that distant era of football history, loyalty was something that could not be measured in cash. Football players were lightyears from being the iconic and fabulously wealthy superheroes of today.

War intervened, and Walker (could we imagine Beckham or Rooney signing up for the battlefronts of Iraq or Afghanistan?) joined the army as a sergeant.

Chelsea signed the Scottish international for £6,000 at the end of hostilities in 1946, and after around 100 appearances for 'The Blues', he travelled north from London to sign again for Hearts (who else?) in December 1948. A Christmas present for the Jambo faithful, desperate to see Tommy Walker once more in maroon. This time he became player/assistant to the manager, Davie McLean, but soon retired to concentrate on management.

McLean's death at the age of 67 in 1951 led to Walker's promotion to manager, and so began Hearts' most successful period in the history of the club. The club that Walker built bulldozed all before it, grabbing all the glittering baubles of Scottish soccer. Starting with the Scottish League Cup in 1955, the club went on to win the Scottish Cup in 1956 and the Scottish League Title of 1957–8 with a record number of goals scored, 132, along with a record goal difference of 103, having lost only 29 goals in 34 games.

In that season (1957–8) Heart of Midlothian swept all before them losing only one match (to Clyde) and drawing four (Kilmarnock, Third Lanark, Clyde and Motherwell). Another Scottish League Cup in 1958 and another Scottish League title in 1959–60 as well as a third Scottish League Cup in the same season soon followed. As a last hurrah, Hearts under Walker won a fourth Scottish League Cup by beating Kilmarnock 1–0 in 1962.

Thomas 'Tommy' Walker OBE died in 1993, five years after my mother. I have happy memories of both, and I am comforted that each, in their own way, will forever haunt Tynecastle.

MASKS AND FACES:
THE STORY OF HARRY BRAHAM

Janet Muir

THERE IS ALWAYS talk of spirits and ghosts, and many people are sceptical, but is there something else, something otherworldly? I now have reason to believe there is...

I have been a volunteer in the Britannia Panopticon Music Hall in Glasgow (where Stan Laurel made his debut) since 2005, and I immediately felt a strange connection when I first entered the building.

I was asked by a friend when I mentioned there had been a comedian in the family, if my relative had appeared there. I didn't know so I started doing some research, and to my delighted amazement found out not only that he had, but also performed before Queen Victoria!

His name was Harry Braham and he was my great, great uncle, but although he was one of the most highly paid and famous Music Hall artistes of his day, his name has passed into obscurity.

Harry was born Henry Nathaniel Braham on 13 September 1850 in St Giles London to Nathaniel Braham and Susan Frost, the eldest of three children. His brother Charles, my direct ancestor, was a Music Hall acrobat (stage name Carl Robarts).

Like many Music Hall artistes of the day Harry became one of The Royal Christy Minstrels, and it was as part of this troupe he performed before HM Queen Victoria at Balmoral Castle on 1 October 1868, singing 'The Royal Wild Beast Show'.

Finding a talent for comic musical characterisations, he left the Minstrels to go solo, naming his act Masks and Faces, making the most of his 'elastic' face and baritone voice.

Following early success in London, an exciting opportunity arose, and at the tender age of 20 he set sail for Adelaide, Australia in August 1871 to join the Foley Troupe with his friend Tommy Hudson, a fellow comedian and champion dancer. They were an instant hit.

Buoyed by this, they left to go to Sydney in January 1872 and played to packed houses at the Café Chantant and School of Arts.

Things were about to change for Harry however, in July of that year he met a well established Irish burlesque singer, named Lizzie

Watson (real name Eliza Hemingway). Romance quickly blos
somed and they married on 6 February 1873 while on tour in
Brisbane.

Harry and Lizzie then formed a duet headlining many times in
Australia and New Zealand throughout 1873 and 1874 with
hundreds of people being turned away each night.

In 1875 they sailed to San Francisco and toured most of the
United States, sometimes performing with the vaudeville impresario
Tony Pastor over the next couple of years. In 1876 Harry created a
solo character act called Silly Bill and Father, the advertising poster
is now considered Retro Art and can be found on T-shirts and mugs

By 1878 they were the highest-paid entertainers of their pro
fession.

Having conquered Australia, New Zealand and America, they
decided to return to Britain in 1879. Undaunted they began getting
bookings and their success continued with the accolade of appearing
at The Crystal Palace on 6 July that year.

Music Hall was a tough occupation which necessitated relent
less touring, and from 23–30 April 1881 they appeared at The Panopticon. By this time however cracks had begun in their relationship
and sadly by the end of that year they had parted.

As a solo act again, Harry was confident in his own talent, and
he was much in demand, appearing with well-known stars of the time
such as Marie Loftus, Dan Leno, Vesta Tilley, Jenny Hill (The Vital
Spark), Arthur Lloyd, Harry Rickards, Charles Coburn, Charles
Sutton, Bessie Bellwood, The Great Vance, and George Leybourne
(the original Champagne Charlie).

In 1883 and again in 1884 his touring included Paris, most likely
at the Moulin Rouge which was the main Music Hall at the time.

In 1887 he toured America with Masks and Faces, and subse
quently started acting in comic plays. One of those in 1890–1 was
The Senator by W.H. Crane in which he starred as the Chinaman
Baron Ling Ching, with Georgia Drew Barrymore, mother of the
famous acting dynasty.

In 1898 he returned to the UK and resumed a heavy touring
schedule, before permanently returning to the USA in 1899.

In 1902 he appeared in *Morocco Bound* based on the book by
Arthur Branscombe.

From February–May 1904 he headlined in Kingston, Jamaica
at the Theatre Royal.

That same year he starred on Broadway as Picorin in the comic opera *Sergeant Kitty*, the main star being Virginia Earle.

In 1906 at the Eden Musee New York he was performing Masks and Faces at the same time that Harry Houdini was at the Vaudeville Theatre. Maybe Harry met Harry, who knows!

Silent films were now becoming more popular, and Harry appeared in three. Two of them, *Suppressed Evidence* in 1912 and *The Fight* in 1915, are now unfortunately presumed lost.

The third however survives and is D.W. Griffiths' controversial 1915 epic *Birth Of A Nation* when he donned blackface once again to play Cameron's servant.

He was still acting on stage and fittingly his last play, Klaw and Erlanger's *Miss Springtime* in 1917 was a massive hit.

Harry then retired to The Actors' Fund Home in New York and died in Staten Island Hospital on 21 September 1923, eight days after his 73rd birthday. His ashes were interred in the actors' plot in Evergreen Cemetery, Brooklyn.

Does fate or destiny play a part in our lives? Sometimes I would like to think so, and, hopefully, I can ensure Harry's name will no longer be forgotten but will live on and he will take his rightful place in Music Hall history.

THINKING OUTSIDE THE BOX

Angus MacDonald

AS A MACDONALD I have heaps of family in the Hebrides, particularly Skye, stretching back for centuries. Although we are now more tenants than owners of these islands, many centuries ago this was not the case, and this story is set in those times.

In these times the MacDonalds and the MacLeods fell out over an island. Both sides had made claims to it, and neither clan would give it up. So, the chieftains of Clan Donald and Clan MacLeod met to debate and decide. Eventually it was decided that, in an effort to avoid bloodshed, a race would be held. The first clan to touch the island would win it. And so the race started, both ships eager to claim their prize.

Both clans strained to coax every knot of speed out of the wind and their sails, the minutes rushing into a brisk glide. Eventually and suddenly, the island appeared, and Clan MacLeod was leading. The MacDonald chieftain called for everything from the men, every ounce of effort in a desperate hope to catch the MacLeods, but it was in vain. Clan MacLeod would touch the island first, and win it. Clan Donald would sail home under a black cloud of shame.

The MacDonald chieftain, my ancestor, wouldn't have this. He quickly made his mind up, ripped his axe from his belt, chopped his hand clean off, and threw it onto the island with his other. Both clans stared in disbelief. Clan Donald had touched the island first, and won.

And that is why, to this day, the badge of Clan Donald shows a hand holding a cross.

THE FIGHT FOR HIS RIGHT

Margaret MacBeath

MY FAMILY LEGEND is my Uncle Albert who fought a long battle to save his family cottage, which was built 120 years ago in Castlecary.

My Uncle Albert (aged 35 at the time) was determined to launch a protest to stop the A80 upgrade going ahead and his house being demolished. The new motorway was going to affect more than 2,000 homes. All my uncle wanted was a stress-free life without worrying that his family home was going to be taken away from him, his wife and their three young boys.

A letter was hand-posted through his door to say his house was getting demolished in January 1994.

He led a high-profile campaign to delay construction work and the planning of the route. He started his campaign by putting a 'Don't demolish our house' sign on the roof of his house the very next day.

He also organised a five-mile protest march, which started at Broadwood Stadium, near Cumbernauld and ended at Castlecary Arches. He then got about 100 of his friends and family to have a sit-down on the main road outside his cottage where the police had to stop the traffic for an hour.

He took the government to court in Edinburgh in 1996, but the government won, and his house was still to be demolished.

In 1998, Labour was now the government and they also wanted to demolish his house.

A public inquiry was held in 2005 where he put forward his case after doing all the legal work himself. He described the government's decision as a complete betrayal of the community. He claimed his family would have to pay a high price for the motorway extension. If the project went ahead it would mean the compulsory purchase and the demolition of my Uncle Albert's much-loved home.

The enquiry decided that the road should still be built, but his house was not to be demolished. This was in June 2006.

The road started to be built in 2008, and then he had to fight to save his 130 trees from being chopped down.

Four trees were chopped down before Aunt Marjory stood in front of the diggers to stop them. This gave Uncle Albert enough time to get the court documents out to show the digger drivers that the trees were not to be chopped down.

He managed to save his home. That's why I think he's an inspiration and also a legend to me and that's why I'm so proud to have him as my uncle. He does everything he sets out to do despite having muscular dystrophy and being wheelchair-bound has never held him back.

When he and the residents decided to make a memorial garden in the field where two girls were sucked into a collapsed mine shaft in 1950, they managed to raise £30,000. They did this by doing sponsored walks, dances and raffles. They also put a new memorial bit into the garden for the train disaster which happened in 1937.

LILIAS OF THE SONG

Colin MacKenzie

MY EIGHT-TIMES-GREAT grandmother, Lilias Campbell, was a beautiful and high-spirited young woman who lived on upper Loch Aweside in the later part of the 18th century. The daughter of a substantial farmer, the tacksman of Achlian, she had no lack of eager suitors.

Prominent among their number was Donald MacNicol, the parish minister of Lismore, who had made her acquaintance when she was visiting relatives on that fertile island, and had fallen deeply in love with her. However, he had a strong rival for her hand in the form of one Captain Campbell of Glen Orchy. Lilias was not the first or the last girl to have her head turned by a scarlet-coated officer with a plausible manner, and she accepted his proposal.

On being told of his rejection, Donald MacNicol sadly took the road for home, and having ridden some distance from Achlian, rested on a hillock where he began to compose a Gaelic lament for his unrequited love. Meanwhile his rival was celebrating his success to an unwise extent.

Flushed with drink and full of self-satisfaction, Captain Campbell called to one of the serving-men of the house, a man considered to be something of a simpleton.

'Come here and give Miss Lilias a kiss, and I will give you a silver shilling!'

The reply that came to this boorish suggestion was not a simpleton's answer.

'I will kiss Miss Lilias right gladly, and look for no reward for it, but only if it should be her will that I should do so.'

At this, Lilias rose and kissed the serving-man, saying, 'You are more of a gentleman than he is! Here is a kiss for you and a shilling also, for showing me the true nature of the man I might have been foolish enough to have married.'

And that was the end of her engagement to Captain Campbell.

Immediately, Lilias sent out a rider, telling him, 'Go quickly after Mr MacNicol, and when you find him say that I ask him to return here, if he will.'

The rider caught up with Donald where he was sitting on the hillock, having just put the finishing touches to his song of loss and longing, and at this news he returned to the house of Achlian a good deal faster than he had left it.

On his arrival, Lilias went out to meet him and spoke to him directly.

'If you have not changed your mind, I have changed mine!'

'Does that mean you will marry me?'

'Yes!'

So Lilias and Donald were married in November 1771 and went to live in the manse of Lismore, where they were happy together and had a large family, but it is only in fairy tales that people live happily ever after. Of their 16 children, no fewer than eight died in early childhood, so they were to have their full share of future sorrow.

As for the minister's lament, it remains to this day in the rich repertoire of Gaelic song.

'*Mo shuil a'd dheigh*' (My eye following thee)

Gone But Not Forgotten

DICK ANDERSON

Kenna Blackhall

WHEN I WAS a young girl – *Dogtanian* was a legend to me – a little cartoon that won the girl, fought the bad guys and rode off into the sunset. When I was a little older, I drew inspiration from Robert the Bruce and William Wallace – legends whose names had been whispered to me from my family like old wives' tales.

Today, I spend less time dreaming and more time drawing on experience from the people in my life that I can learn from and admire. The type of people who show you how to live your life simply by seeing the grace in which they live theirs.

So when the email inviting stories popped up in my inbox, I thought of obvious legends to write about; my mum (a famous poet), my dad (a retired army man) or perhaps my brother (a troubled past)... Nothing seemed to ring true, until the least obvious story stood out as the story to tell. After all, there is only one grave that I visit twice a year and only one person who shares the name of the man I love.

His passing was sudden, unexpected and devastating. And the reason why one regular day, a boy boarded a flight home with a heavy heart, and landed a man. A woman woke as a wife and went to sleep a widow, a daughter lost her father, and a young girl her childhood with a devoted grandparent. One day he was alive, and the next he was gone. No-one could say goodbye. For this family, tomorrow never came.

Seven years have now passed since his death. His family has grown up, and life has moved on. But every day in small and sometimes large ways his absence is noted – at the dinner table, a special birthday, when a fridge requires fixing or a heart needs mending.

Perhaps it's not my story to tell – I never met Dick after all. I never saw his hairy moustache, or witnessed the kindness and support that he provided to everyone in his life. I wasn't there when he used his joinery skills to make a home for his son and I didn't see him mentor the young apprentices that worked for him (although I did read the amazing things they wrote about him).

I didn't see his face filled with fear at the thought of flying or the pride in his eyes when he watched his granddaughter play. And

I wasn't at the church to see the hundreds of mourners that came to pay their respects at his passing.

I was nevertheless there after his death and I do see the legacy that he has left behind. And although he is gone, each year, I get to know him a little better – brought to life through the eyes of the family that knew and loved him so dearly. Living on through the people he loved.

We all walk through life surrounded by legends and our memories and stories ensure they are not forgotten. So this is the story of Dick Anderson – a real life legend.

DAD

Anneliese Mackintosh

MR PONKY, his gravestone reads.

Except it isn't a gravestone, it's a wooden heart. And the writing is made of fridge magnet letters, stuck on with superglue.

Technically speaking, it's not his grave, either. It's a Foxwhelp apple tree, and a few of his ashes are beneath the roots. Ashes made up of his eyes, hair, teeth; made up of the tangled sentences of the last letter I ever wrote to him.

He was cremated on Friday the 13th. The ashes were still hot when we poured them into his wellington boots. I took the right boot and Mum took the left, and we went around the garden, scattering. It was windy outside, and we choked back tears – and bits of my father – as thick grey gusts of him blew into our noses and mouths. Afterwards we drank Cava and ate fish and chips. We chewed our nails and tugged at our hair and said we hope it's what he would have wanted. Yes, yes, we said, in turns. It is what he would have wanted: the second we finished sprinkling his ashes, the sun came out. That was his way of telling us.

In truth, though, it was difficult to say what Dad would have wanted. Mainly because there were so many different sides to him. For every different side he had a different name. His full name was plentiful in itself: Alastair Anthony Hugh Fraser Mackintosh. But he was also known as Mr Ponky. And Bananaman. And Just William. And Skippy the Bush Kangaroo. And all the other characters and creatures he pretended to be whilst jumping around the kitchen table first thing in the morning. 'Dad, Dad!' my sister and I would sing. 'Do Skippy, Dad! Do Bananaman!'

The last time I saw him alive, he wasn't any of those characters. He wasn't even himself. He was an old man at 56, wrapped in a woollen blanket on a patio sun lounger. It was 5.30 in the morning, and he was crying. 'Goodbye sweetheart,' he said quietly. 'Go on lots of adventures for me.'

But my dad's definition of 'adventures' is going to be hard to live up to. When he was a student he took off all his clothes – all of them – and ran around his university campus completely naked.

He phoned the press beforehand then was interviewed by the local paper whilst standing nude in the union bar.

I could go on.

Eventually, my father got kicked out of university.

Then he went back to university and got a First-Class Honours followed by a PhD.

The PhD was in Electronic Engineering, and it was something to do with improving image processing in CAT scans, for detecting cancer. At the same time as finishing his PhD, Dad was designing satellites for the European Space Agency in Germany. This is where I was born: Anneliese Sabine, a German souvenir.

Back in the UK, Daddy became a Doctor Daddy. That's what I boasted at his graduation. 'It's a Doctor Daddy. My Doctor Daddy. Doctor Daddy was very clever indeed, and he went on to design something called Taxi, which was a graphical user interface for early computers.

Taxi was really what gave Dad the ride of his life. To publicise it, he did a fancy photo shoot for *The Times*, wearing a white top hat and tails, jumping out of a big black cab. After that, Taxi took him on numerous trips around the world, from Tokyo to Silicon Valley. We even ended up living in California for a few months – Mum, Dad, me, and my new baby sister, Kirsten Laura.

After America, Dad was invited to do some promotional talks with two other men in London. Each of them, like my dad, had designed a graphical user interface, and this was the opportunity for the three of them to show off what they'd got. The first interface was called GEM for Digital Research. The second interface was called Windows for Microsoft.

You might have heard of it.

Well, to cut a long story short, Taxi never shot to fame. Microsoft Windows, as I'm sure you know, did. The company that my Dad worked for began focusing – very successfully – on printers instead of operating systems, so Taxi took a back seat, and finally its journey ended altogether.

A few years later, Dad set up his own company. He always valued programming above paperwork, so the business didn't run as smoothly as it might have done, but it did okay. It did well.

Dad never forgot about Taxi, though, and the life he nearly had. He'd sometimes get tears in his eyes and apologise for being a failure, which amazed me because I didn't think he was a failure at all. He was my absolute hero. Not because of his career, as it happens, even though that impressed me. He was my hero because of the way he jumped around the kitchen table first thing in the morning. Because of how often he made me smile.

And I don't give two hoots about the person that my dad never managed to become. In fact, I feel like the luckiest person in the world to have known the person – and the people – that he was. And luckier still that I can call that person, and those people, Dad.

Larger Than Life

BILLY'S FAMILY LEGEND

Billy London

MY FATHER IS MY choice for the legend in our family. He was always organising things for other people. I remember when I was five and we lived in Garthamlock, my dad organised a trip to see *Snow White* in a local pub. All the weans in the scheme were there and everybody loved it. It's something I've never forgotten because we were all so happy and the atmosphere was great. Nobody was arguing or fighting and it seemed like a magic time.

He also volunteered with the Salvation Army but he wasn't really religious himself. I remember him organising trips to the seaside, to places like Ayr. He helped to organise other things for the local kids like Christmas parties. My da was a bit of a tough guy I think because he never let us away with anything like being cheeky to adults or answering back. He used to say 'Kids should be seen and not heard.'

If we spoke when adults were talking, we would be sent out to play or told, 'Go to your room.'

He was big on discipline because of his time in the Navy. He worked on minesweepers but I don't remember him talking much about it. I think he wanted to forget about those days but I don't know why. Maybe he saw some bad things or stuff that he did not want to remember. I remember my sister telling us that one day her class had to stand up and tell everyone about their dad. She stood up and said, 'My da killed hunners of Germans.'

The teacher asked if it was true and for all we knew it was.

An interesting thing is that he used to play billiards for money. He was a great player and played in a club called Smokey Joe's somewhere in Glasgow. Sometimes the guys he beat couldn't pay him so they gave him their cues. I remember when I was wee he had a big collection of cues in the bedroom. When I was older I heard lots of stories about him and other women but he always came home to my ma.

Although he never earned big money he liked to wear the best of gear and was a right snappy dresser. Maybe his billiard money helped buy the good suits and stuff he had. A funny thing I remember was that he kept his wardrobe locked all the time. It was a bit mysterious and even my ma never got to open it.

I remember years later talking to other folk who were at th Snow White film who said they had always remembered it as wel They said the atmosphere was brilliant and couldn't believe ho the local gangs had stopped fighting and how people cam together. It was the first time some of the kids had seen a film on big screen because the area was very poor but everybod remembered the free crisps and juice that were laid on. Some guy said they loved the club atmosphere that much that they wanted t grow up quicker so they could drink and feel that atmospher again.

I would say my da was a real character. Everybody in the schem knew him. He was well liked and respected for the things he di He always tried to do things for other people, but his Snow Whit film was the thing that folk remember to this day. For that reaso I think my dad is definitely our family's legend.

GREAT AUNT KATE

Sheila Masson

GREAT AUNT KATE was a ghost from another world, another generation. Her life would be defined by her gender and her era.

'She was a woman of her time, very much so,' said my Aunty Mary, 'she always struck me as a very sad little woman.'

Aunty Kate was born Catherine Elizabeth Wallace in Edinburgh in 1888, the only sister to seven brothers. While the boys were educated at the best schools in the area, Kate was made to leave school early, at 14 or younger.

'She definitely was not happy that she was the one who was made to leave school,' said my Aunty Jane.

Furthermore, any passing interest that she showed in a boy was belittled by her brothers. When she met Mr King, a gentleman friend whom she wanted to marry, her brothers refused to allow her to do so, on the grounds that he wasn't good enough for her. So instead of choosing her own life to live, with a husband, family and career, it was Great Aunt Kate's duty to look after her ageing parents and to help her brothers with their children.

However, despite there being more successful, prolific and even famous relatives, it is Aunty Kate who appears more frequently in anecdotes. These tales elicit groans and giggles from her grand nieces and nephews, the last children she looked after, who are now in their 60s and 70s. In particular her culinary skills were legendary.

'Her cooking was terrible,' said Aunty Jane. 'She would take a chicken and put it in a pot of boiling water. Absolutely ghastly. She was also very into making potted meat.'

This dish was known as 'potted heid', according to Aunty Christine.

'It was a pork thing,' she said, 'jellied odds and ends all pressed together in gelatin. Revolting. At Christmas time she would often bring a kind of carrot pudding, a steamed pudding. She loved to come and pick the elderberries because we had elderberry bushes in the allotment. And she would make elderberry jam. We used to tease her and say that she was making elderberry wine.'

Two of Great Aunt Kate's nephews were doctors who frequently

travelled away from home, leaving their spinster aunt in charge o
the various children, three in one family and four in another.

'We tended to rebel against her regimes,' said Uncle Alistair, 'i
was the same old thing, day in, day out. I wasn't the instigator. W
were doing it collectively.'

Alistair's cousin Jane added, 'She came and looked after us whe
we were really quite small. I remember it was when I had my firs
cigarette! I was about five. (My brother) Ian and his friend used t
buy Woodbines singly at the newsagents and they bribed me wit
a cigarette not to tell Aunty Kate. She used to read *People's Friend*
which was like Mills & Boon,' added Jane, 'that's how I learne
the facts of life!'

'Staying with Aunty Kate, it was a simple life – fairly austere,
said Uncle Alistair. 'She spoke very slowly and quietly. It was always
"Helloooo?"'

That was our joke, if Aunty Kate was on the phone it wa
always, 'Helloooo?'

We all tended to tease her behind her back.

She was a tiny, thin woman with dark, greying, tousled hair.

'She was almost conservative Victorian in her style,' said Uncl
Alistair. 'She was never one for looking at fashion, she never wor
makeup.'

'I always remember her shoes,' said Aunty Mary, 'Louis Quinz
kitten-heeled shoes, with little buttons, like button hooks.'

'She wore dark clothes,' added Aunty Jane, 'nothing very bright
She strongly disapproved when a Littlewoods, or something down
market like that, opened on Princes Street, and the girls there wer
wearing nail polish! She though that this was absolutely dreadful.

'She was rather prim,' agreed Jane's brother Ian. 'She wa
brought up in the age of Queen Victoria, she was of that kind o
vintage. The boundaries were very clearly drawn. She dressed i
clothes that would be classed as very dated, very long skirts an
boots with button hooks with a wee curly end to it. Black leathe
shoes with a small heel and a strap that came over with a butto
and hole. It was dated even then, this was the 1950s. She wa
barely five foot tall in her high heels. She knitted stockings wit
four knitting needles, she made her own, and repaired then
obviously. I did recall she did not go out without a hat on. The hat
I remember were close-fitting and held in place with hat pins. The

ould be around three inches long and no doubt, would now be
onsidered offensive weapons.'

'She always wore long heavy overcoats and her skirts were
lways long,' said Uncle Alastair, 'almost ankle length, dark tweed.
remember having a chuckle at her washing line with her long white
nickers hanging there, bloomer-type things, very baggy.'

She is also remembered lying in bed, singing hymns to herself,
aving found solace in religion, or rather, spiritualism, attending
piritualist meetings in Edinburgh. Aunty Mary remembers a spooky
noment.

'When I got engaged, Aunty Kate said, "I've been speaking to
our granddad and he's so pleased for you." This was 18 months
fter he died!'

The grand nieces and nephews were aware of the limitations of
heir great aunt's life and the sad situation with Mr King, her thwarted
oyfriend, as throughout her life they still met up, albeit in very
ormal settings. Neither of them ever married and some time before
er death in 1972, at the age of 83, Aunty Kate said of Mr King,
I've never felt the same since my friend died.'

MY MOTHER'S HAIR IS RED

Katy McAulay

MY MUM'S GRADUATION photo sits on the sideboard of a bungalow in Bonnyrigg. This is her parents' house, a modest prize bought with the fruits of my grandad's labour down the coal mines. Like many of the pictures thronging the living room, this one was taken before the days of colour photography. Although Mum is displayed in black and white, you can still tell she's ginger.

Now she's a beautiful woman, and clever with it, but sometimes I wonder if that was enough to stop her from being bullied when she was younger. At my school, she would have been called a 'ginger'. She would have been called 'minging'. She would have been asked if her pubes were carrot too.

My hair is brown, like Bourneville. And my eyes, when I was a baby, they were so dark they were almost black. Nonetheless, if you were to lift the cocoa mass of my mane and examine the underside, or if I were to tie it into a ponytail, you'd see that two sections stretching back from my temples betray my redhead heritage. It's Bourneville right enough, but the ginger nut is fighting to get through.

Luckily, it was easy to keep my auburn streaks a secret all the way through school. My disappointments and knocks, when they came, were bad skin and wonky teeth, a bout of glandular fever that exhausted me, hollowed me out, leaving only sadness behind. Fortunately I had a conscientious doctor, one who informed us that depression following this sort of illness was common, so it didn't cause undue concern. All the same, I can remember walking through the school gates each day at four and getting into my mum's car; she'd turn and ask how I was and then I'd begin to weep.

'What's wrong?' she'd say. 'Tell me what's wrong.'

I'd shake my head. There was nothing wrong. Nothing except for the misery I felt, and no end to it in sight. My mum fixed it, as mums often do. She was wary of pills and prescriptions, wary of pandering to illness at all, but she did some research and presented me with a bottle of St John's Wort. A sprinkle of this twice daily and within a month, I was singing. This was just as well, because my

198

mum didn't approve of taking sick days. She was a teacher then, business studies and economics, and she didn't like seeing learning disrupted.

Her method of ensuring good results, she told me once, involved sizing up each new class on their first day. She'd let them sit where they wanted, watch for the troublemakers and the shy, the ones who needed help and the ones who'd shine without her intervention. During the second lesson, she'd introduce a seating plan. Re-ordering her pupils into a pattern of her own choosing thwarted their attempts to steal focus from the matter in hand, she said. And that matter was important. That matter was understanding opportunity cost and the division of labour. It was being awarded a credit grade, when everyone said you were only fit for a general. Mum's always been good at showing others how to get the best out of themselves.

True, meeting her standards hasn't always been easy.

'You know you can look very pretty,' she told me recently, 'if you'd only make an effort.'

I remember, years ago, finding myself banished to my teenage bedroom, my ears burnt by maternal ire because I'd waltzed home with a love bite on my neck after a day spent in the park with a boy she didn't rate.

'You're like a bitch in heat,' she said.

It's still shocking to me that my mother, my bus-pass-carrying mother; my Marks and Spencer's shopping, Christmas-cake-making, practically teetotal mother, could have uttered something so offensive. Mind you, I can barely believe that she was a smoker for five years either, or that she ever wore aviator sunglasses, or had a perm, drove 'a wee convertible', or hurled a frying pan at my dad during an argument.

She did all of that, and more. It was the redhead in her coming out. It was all of those other things that she could have been; musician, chef, doctor, entrepreneur, rushing to the surface and fighting to be seen.

She could have succeeded in any number of professions. I know it. She was the first in her family to go to university, the first to have a graduation photograph to display on the sideboard at all, and although many career paths were open to her, she decided to be a teacher, to help others to make it to university too. I'm proud that she did, and grateful. Her former pupils must feel tha gratitude too.

Mum's 61 now, though on a good day, you'd think her close to 50. On her bus pass photo, her hair appears blonde. She's bee toning it down for years, gradually preparing for the grey. But th red's still there.

I glimpse it when she arrives on my doorstep armed wit flowers and homemade soup. It comes to the surface when sh helps my granddad organise his bewildering array of medical appoin ments, or dispenses first-rate fashion advice, or chooses a Kin Creosote album for the car and turns it up full volume. And blazed on the day of my brother's wedding, when she danced 'Stri the Willow' and was determined to stand in the snow afterward even without an umbrella, waiting to shower the departing coupl with confetti.

I wore my hair up that day, decided to give the ginger streak an airing. Now, looking at the photographs of mum and me, I'm smiling, and I'm finding that I want to run to her side. I want t lean in close and tell her, 'Let the red come through, Mum. Fryin pans may fly, but we love it in you, because it's who you are.'

In the end, it's who I am, too.

AUNTY BEA IS FULL OF SHOCK!

Karen Taylor

OUR FAMILY LEGEND is my Aunty Bea. Bold and beautiful, extrovert and warm, funny and engaging, she was born with the gift of the gab and an open personality which endears her to all those she comes into contact with. Aunty Bea is 'full of shock' is how my two-year-old cousin aptly described her. Her crazy stories, based on real-life escapades, have kept our family enthralled and in fits of laughter for six decades now.

Born in Trinidad in 1948, she was, like all the best people, a mistake. The result of an unplanned pregnancy resulting in a third daughter for Sarah and Fred. Stories from her early childhood in the West Indies include the times she was locked in the chicken coop as punishment by her father, her on-going battles with a feisty cockerel who always attacked her, the nickname 'Silverhead' she earned from the time she fled across the garden to escape an injection from the district nurse and the time she smacked her sister round the head with a metre ruler just because she was 'being too quiet'.

Her father tried to 'cure' her fear of snakes by trapping one in a large glass jar and leaving it on the dining table as the family ate their meals. She was tubby as a child and earned the nickname 'Podge' until a love of British confectionery, discovered in the Welsh post office of her brother-in-law's family, developed into an obsession and she finally sickened herself from sweet things for the rest of her life. From the podgy pre-teen an impossibly attractive glamour-puss emerged and her many and varied encounters with members of the opposite sex ensued. Tall, slim, blonde, with big made-up eyes, trendy clothes and huge earrings (she was like the human embodiment of my Sindy doll), she made an impact on Tom Jones who spotted her in the audience of Top of the Pops at Granada TV in the 60s and held her hand as he sang from the stage. She'd painted her fingernails black with white exclamation marks on them especially for the show.

My mother, who was married by now and living in Abu Dhabi, remembers many a night fending off the lonely bachelors of the oil industry from Bea's allure when she came to visit. Mum used to put a protective sun-hat over Bea's boobs as she lay on the beach in her itsy-bitsy bikini. One night, after a dance at the club, she got driven off into the desert where her seducer drugged her 'chaperone' with strong whisky and then proceeded to open his suitcase, revealing it to be packed only with raw steak and champagne. In the end she married a Jamaican called Keith and I was flower girl at her wedding in the mid-70s. The couple settled in Jamaica where Bea ended up teaching pop stars Althea and Donna of 'Uptown Top Ranking' fame and making friends with Miss Jamaica, subsequently Miss World 1976 and Bob Marley's girlfriend, Cindy Breakspeare. Bea remembers visiting the Marley residence with Cindy where the great artist himself sat smoking huge ganga spliffs rolled in newspapers.

The wild parties, where everybody inevitably ended up in the pool in various states of undress, continued through the 1970s until civil unrest in the country reared its ugly head. Bea was held up when driving by masked men brandishing guns and had to hide in her bedroom while armed intruders ransacked her home. Several of her friends were raped. The strain took its toll and her marriage broke down in a sea of debt. She moved to Toronto in the 1980s. More adventures ensued in her new environment. She made friends with rodeo riders with strange names like 'Hoover' and, inadvertently, with an ex-murderer who took the same subway to work as her every day. She moved to Calgary to be nearer my mother, who now lived there, and drove a bright yellow Ford Mustang car which she called 'Woodstock' after the Peanuts character. Bea's cars always had names and she cried when she came to sell them. From this point Bea became part of our everyday family life, popping in to visit on the way home from work each day and sink a few 'sundowners' with my parents.

Sadly, the party lifestyle of her youth, plus a genetic predisposition, had led to a dependence on alcohol which crept up imperceptibly over the years. These were the years of the 'midnight feasts'. Bea would eat hardly anything all day, she was forever watching her figure in case she should return to the days of 'Podge' but would come down to the kitchen in the middle of the night and cook the most extraordinary things, almost in her sleep. I'll never forget the time I found her heating up tomato soup with Monster Munch crisps bobbing about in it! She followed my family to Scotland in the late 1980s and eventually beat her alcoholism but not before putting us all through the mill by drinking herself into a coma.

Aunty Bea is 'full of shock' as my toddler cousin had once said. Of course, being Bea, she had to take it to extremes. Her coma registered three on the Glasgow Coma Scale, no response to pain, no eye movement, no speech. Thankfully, after a bleak few days when we imagined we'd lost her, she pulled through and has remained on the wagon ever since. She now sponsors others who are struggling with addiction and has settled into a quiet life at last where she plays tennis, walks, works, loves her TV and *Daily Express*, drinks vats of Diet Coke, meets friends for lunch and attends her meetings. I'm so proud of her for overcoming the addiction that plagued her for many years and so happy to have her as my fun-loving, story-telling, wonderful aunt. She's been like the big sister I never had and is truly a family legend.

THE HOWDIE-WIFE

Anne Ewing

JOHANN BARCLAY MITCHELL was my great granny. Although she died 12 years before I was born, I have always felt connected to her through the many vivid recollections of her that my mother shared with me. As privileged recipients of the best of the oral tradition in the passing down of family story and folk memory, I and my own family in turn, have felt enriched by the opportunity to gain some insight into the lives of preceding generations. These glimpses of my great granny's life and the world she inhabited led me to have a great admiration for her and the place she occupied in the life of her family and of the wider community. I am three generations distant from her, and live in a world vastly different from the one she knew, and yet I am only too aware of the influence she had on succeeding generations.

Hann was the howdie-wife in the small town of Markinch in Fife, where she helped to deliver the babies and tended to the sick and dying. As was usual in the early years of the twentieth century, most communities relied on the services of women like her who, although they had no formal nursing qualifications, acted as mid-wives and nurses in cooperation with the medical practitioners who also served those communities. As she shared deep life and death experiences with the people she lived amongst, she grew to be highly respected and valued by them.

Every Sunday in the summer Hann, dressed in a clean black dress and a freshly laundered and starched white apron, would take a stroll through the town. As she went, she would help herself to a bloom from the occasional garden, returning home with a lovely floral bouquet! No-one objected, perhaps because this was a way for the townsfolk to acknowledge the debt they owed to this woman who had brought most of the bairns into the world and would see many of the folk out, hopefully, but sadly not always, as old men and women. Others would die as children and young adults from virulent infantile diseases like diphtheria, scarlet fever or meningitis or from the scourge of tuberculosis. I assume she was paid for her work, but whether this came directly from her clients or indirectly from the family doctors I have no way of knowing.

My great granny must have witnessed much grief, heartache and hardship, and indeed had personal experience of all three. She herself lost a son at seven years of age and a granddaughter at a few months old. She saw one son emigrate to Canada with his young family, and another to Australia. Her last few years witnessed the hungry times of the Great Depression. Poor people still had an innate fear of the 'puir's hoose', and the lack of any kind of social security safety net meant that all their waking hours were spent in a ceaseless struggle to make ends meet and maintain the basic wherewithal for survival.

On my mother's first day at work in the Balbirnie Wool Mill at 14 years of age, she and other new girls had to give their names to the wages clerk. When four of them, including my mother, gave their Christian names as 'Johann' he replied, 'So, ye're a' Hann Barclay's bairns!' He knew that they had all been delivered by, and named after, my great granny. I know my mother always felt an appreciation of the legacy her granny left her, and an impulse to live up to the example she set her as she struggled to overcome the hardships and rise to the many challenges she was faced with throughout her life.

After she lost her husband Jeck in 1932, Hann would often say 'Ah, but Ah miss yer faither'. Two years later she took ill, and right away began to persist in a refusal to accept medical treatment or to take nourishment. Attempts by the doctor to persuade her did no good and in fact were met with a stern instruction, 'An' nane o' yer needles, mind!' Pleas from her family were similarly ignored as she explained, 'That wid be a great peety, noo that Ah've come this faur.' It seemed that she had made up her mind to die and would not be denied her desire to be gone. She was granted her wish and died a peaceful and dignified death a short time later.

A final testament to the respect and affection in which Hann was held by the people of Markinch, came with her funeral. In those days Sunday funerals were common and hers coincided with Armistice Day, 11 November. The mourners came on to her burial in St Drostan's cemetery from the remembrance service at the war memorial on Markinch Hill. Her coffin was carried by 'her bairns', all young men she had brought into the world. I wonder how many others had tragically been killed in the Great War, and so could not be there that day, to perform a service to a woman who had been so closely identified with the community she served.

KEITH – TRUE GRIT

Trezann

HE WAS BORN on a murky March morning and his entry into the world was to change that world, not just for his family, but for a great many people. A sickly child, he was written off by most people, but he was a fighter. Twice he was on the point of death with serious illnesses, but he pulled through. He needed more care and attention than his older brother but was soon reaching his developmental milestones, albeit a little later than others. He was carried up his first Munro (a Scottish mountain over 3,000 ft) in a papoose by his granddad at age two and 'bagged' his first one, Beinn Ghlas, unaided, aged six. It was the first of many. He walked every step of the way. The promise of a Mars Bar at the top always served to encourage him to keep going and his jaunty little figure striding ahead always seemed to serve as a reminder to Mum that she had to keep going too. He continued to accompany the family on climbing and walking trips in the Scottish mountains and the Lake District in all weathers and, on more than one occasion, drew gasps of amazement from others who had struggled to reach the heights he did. Once on the summit of Helvellyn in the Lake District, a group of young army squaddies appeared over the horizon, exhausted and sweating. Their speechlessness owed more to their astonishment at seeing Keith there than to their lack of fitness. When they had got their breath back they asked 'how did he get here?' to which I replied, 'same as you, he walked and climbed.' They were mightily impressed.

As a teenager he swapped two feet for two wheels and proceeded to cycle the length and breadth of the British Isles, accompanied by his father on week-long trips staying in youth hostels and camping. On one occasion Keith, his dad and big brother had just cycled round Loch Tay, some 35 miles' slog of up hill and down dale. At one stage while going down a steep hill his hat blew off and in trying to catch it he wobbled and fell off his bike. Both his palms were scraped raw, not to mention his knees (this is where 'True Grit' comes in) but he insisted on finishing the trip. Even a visit to the Chemist in Killin, who advised giving up, did not deter him. He climbed back in the saddle. On arriving back at our starting point at Kenmore we were all exhausted, physically and emotionally (well, I was emotional). Keith immediately challenged his brother to a game of tennis! He loved to compete and was always determined to win. Nothing kept him down for long.

Keith's skill and aptitude for cycling saw him represent his region and his country on many occasions and he was soon winning competitions – three gold medals, a silver, a bronze and many others. When he gave up cycling he progressed to four legs and began horse riding. Again, the same dogged determination saw him compete in many competitions and he won prizes for dressage and stable management. I thought I was going to burst with pride the first time I saw him compete in dressage at Gleneagles. He was so handsome and elegant on that horse. He was in complete control. A gold medal was forthcoming for stable management.

School was a challenge for Keith, just as it is for many children, but he applied the same single-minded determination to his lessons and on leaving undertook a four year course at college. This involved some very complicated bus changes and timing but as before, Keith took everything in his stride. He coped admirably and was a popular and well-liked student.

A work placement in a McDonald's restaurant was the stuff of dreams for Keith and on completion of the placement and his college course he was offered permanent employment. That was 19 years ago and he still works there, impressing staff and customers alike with his good humour and his willingness to work hard.

Recently I was diagnosed with a very serious illness and Keith again rose to the challenge. He decided it was his responsibility to undertake the family's entire laundry needs. He gathered, sorted, washed, hung out and brought in washing and helped his dad out with all manner of household tasks. His love and care were instrumental in my recovery and he never complained or looked for thanks or recognition.

Keith's cheerfulness and good nature, and his determination to try anything and not to give up in the face of sometimes overwhelming obstacles, has made him a legend not only in our family but much further afield. He has inspired many individuals and families by his influence and example to soldier on even when all around are saying 'it can't be done'. As a result of the privilege of knowing him, many of his cousins and other family members and friends have taken up jobs in areas of employment that they might never have considered. He has been an inspiration, an educator, a role model and a source of great love, pride and joy to not only his immediate family but to all who come in contact with him. He is indeed a legend. We call him 'True Grit'.

Oh, by the way, did I mention that Keith has Down's Syndrome?

THE LEGEND THAT IS MY MOTHER

Nancy Clusker

MY MOTHER WAS born on 13 September 1911. She grew up as a grey-eyed blonde, her hair so pale that people said it was like lint.

When she met my father she was 17. She forever recalled walking in the evenings to the start of White's Road, eager for the sight of his lean frame silhouetted against the wooden frame, waiting for her. They married and before my mother was 19 their first son was born. They lived in a cottage outside Westfield, life was hard but happy. Washing was done in the wash house; stone steps scrubbed and the outside toilet bleached. Pails of milk were carried from the farm and rugs beaten until they gave up their stour.

When their second son died of diphtheria, the loss turned the young couple into sombre shadows of themselves. It was a relief to escape the memories and move house back into the village with their son and two little girls. Gradually happiness seeped back, and another baby was expected.

On 2 November 1941 my father left for the night shift at Hassockrigg Colliery. He was killed by a falling rock in the early hours of 3 November. My mother kept a cutting of the lines from a poem.

'We never know we go – when we are going
We jest and shut the door;
Fate following behind us, bolts it
And we accost no more.'

The pits were not nationalised. A sum of money was allocated for the young man's life, and doled out weekly to his widow. Stricken with grief, and with a new baby, she kept going somehow, relying on thrift and ingenuity to eke out a living for her family. Time, daily routine and small distractions assuaged the pain.

Mum always made sure there was money for us to go to the pictures in the Miner's Welfare. The pictures opened another world for us, and for her. Another distraction was Mr Seigal, in homburg and black coat, who travelled from Glasgow. He tried to persuade our mum to buy a blouse or a cardigan for herself, but it was cross-over pinnies she mulled over, which she wore every day. But in July 1947, my mother bought a tweed coat in McNaughtons in Bathgate. It cost £19.95 and a down payment of £8 was made. The balance was paid off monthly and cleared a year later. Oh the mad extravagance of it! She kept the receipt, a burr on her conscience for years.

In 1947 also, a hamper arrived from Princess Elizabeth after her marriage to Prince Philip. The gift acknowledged our mother's struggle. We stood, tentatively fingering the parcels from a princess. Our mother read the note and wept.

The note, the receipt, poems, letters, snippets of comfort from magazines were squirreled away and placed in her Promise Box. And on long, lonely Sundays my mother would read them. Bereft as she was they were solace for her soul.

But from reverie she steeled herself time and time again. She composed a fine letter to an organisation which helped distressed gentlewomen, but distressed though she was, she was not gentlewoman enough. Just as well, for it was her feisty character that helped her to survive.

As we grew up, perhaps because of our mother's beauty and sense of style, she was drawn to shops and fashion. Even with no money she danced us three girls round Glasgow shops; Pettigrew and Stephens, Copeland and Lye and Dalys in Sauchiehall Street, and MacDonalds in Buchanan Street. She knew the price of everything, and the value. Organdie, seersucker, chiffon, grosgrain were words that tripped off her tongue as she fingered the materials reverently. Duck egg blue, eau de nil, ashes of roses taught the nuance of colour. Leg of mutton sleeves, sweetheart necklines, smocking adored all the more because they were unattainable. Once, filling in a table of family likes and dislikes, I asked my mother what her favourite dress was. She never missed a beat. 'The autumn brown taffeta.' We gazed at each other, the words bewitched us.

Our mother was ahead of her time. In the '60s when a local worthy asked why she encouraged a daughter to go to university, she looked him in the eye. 'Education is easily carried,' she replied crisply.

Through her years, high levels of expertise were demanded from tradesmen who crossed her threshold, her hawk eyes never missed a piece of shoddy workmanship. She paid every workman on the nail, albeit grudgingly, every penny a prisoner.

With the ascendency of Mrs Thatcher, Mum developed a great

interest in politics, enjoying the cut and thrust and the Prime Minister's haughty assurance. Moreover there was Mrs T's wardrobe; jewellery, hats, handbags, outfits all scrutinised. Were they not both 'iron ladies'?

Mum had holidays abroad and zipped up and down to London. She tripped resplendent to grandchildren's graduations in Glasgow and Edinburgh and sauntered down the Royal Mile, heels striking the cobbles in proclamation. Then at 90 years old at her granddaughter's wedding smiling, her hat a concoction of black gauze and silk feathers.

In 2002 Mum, ever the fighter, brought the circumstances of her husband's death to Brian Wilson, the Minister of State. Our father had not died of respiratory disease and she hoped against hope that some compensation might be paid. None was, but Mr Wilson acknowledged the 'inordinate struggle' which she had endured at that time. That was enough for her.

Shortly before she died in 2006 my mother, then 94, pondered, 'I didn't know I was a single mother, that's what they are called now. I was just a widow with children.'

Reluctantly she let go of the life she had won back.

I remember gorgeous eyes turned gimlet, looking up from the newspaper. 'There are things that will ALWAYS flatter a woman, fur, pearls and velvet! You remember that, will ye?'

I remember that. And so much more.

COBRA

Arthur Clark

MY FATHER WAS born in Glasgow, grew up in the Great Depression of the 1930s, endured the Blitz, and after the war would come home on a Friday night from his job in the shipyards, change, get out his Raleigh bicycle and cycle out of the bomb-damaged city to breathe the sweet country air of the Trossachs; or he would pedal across to Campbeltown, spending the weekend in a little tent and cooking his meals on a camp fire. His summer holidays, the Glasgow Fair fortnight, would be spent 'doon the water' at Rothesay.

In the winter time his weekend evenings would be spent playing in his accordion band at dances in the town. This was how he met my mother, who was a keen dancer and had a good singing voice.

They got married and as the years passed my mother gave birth in turn to four boys. This meant that my father could no longer spend his weekends in his beloved countryside. Money was tight and he had to sell his bike and camping gear.

Then an opportunity arose to move to the country permanently. An advertisement in the *Glasgow Herald* by the Forestry Commission offered jobs to fit and healthy men to work in their afforestation programme in the Highlands. He got the job, and we were off. My mother, a Glasgow 'keelie' through and through, was not so keen.

The house we moved to had a large garden and fenced-off wooded area adjoining, with a lively stream running through it.

An adventure playground for small, city boys.

This treescape became known as the Hen Run, and although it is empty now save for birds and squirrels, and the hen house and sheds are dilapidated and rotting, it is still referred to by the family as such.

My father, clueless as to the actuality of country living, decided to buy some hens. My mother was pleased at the thought of fresh eggs every day to feed her growing boys. She could be heard singing happily in the kitchen. Through an ad in the *Exchange and Mart* (the country man's Bible) he ordered 20 'point of lay' hens, which duly arrived in crates on the back of an Albion lorry and were introduced to their new home.

Time passed and I can remember my mother complaining about the lack of promised eggs. My father assured her that it would not be long now.

'I will increase their corn feed,' he said. 'They will likely be needing more roughage to form the shells.'

Bucket loads of corn later, they had not produced a single egg, although the birds continued to grow with combs of fire engine red contrasting with their snowy white plumage.

The eggless mystery was solved unexpectedly in the dawn of a new summer's day. A cacophony of discordant sound erupted suddenly from the hen house. Twenty lusty thoughts greeted the sunrise as though competing for a prise. Twenty impostors who would not and could not lay an egg supposing they devoured fields of golden corn. Twenty beautiful red combed cockerels proclaimed their new-found puberty – and not a hen for miles!

My mother angrily upbraided my father, 'Ah telt ye there was something funny aboot thay hens.'

As time went on the cockerels, or cullochs as they were called in the Highlands, reduced steadily in numbers as they went for the pot. Their numbers dwindled until at last only one remained, the strongest and healthiest bird of the original 20. More hens were bought at point of lay and some already laying. The breed's name was Rhode Island Red, reputed to be the best layers. My mother was delighted. It showed. She was singing again, my father accompanying her on his accordion. He too was happy.

But, all was not well in the hen run. The remaining cockerel, whom we had named 'Cobra' after his disconcerting tendency of thrusting out his long neck and striking, snake-like at whatever and whoever had displeased him or threatened his harem, ruled the roost, both hen and human.

I can see him now, heckles raised, his extended neck and fearful beak, huge wings batting the ground as he charged at me in one of his fearful displays of tyranny.

But at last, as with all despots, he went too far. A vicious attack on my mother as she fed the hens their midday meal resulted in a death sentence.

When my father returned from work he was told in no uncertain terms to 'wring that damned cockerel's neck.'

My father set off for the hen run, us children trailing behind in anticipation. Dad was going to kill Cobra. His execution was not to be missed. Not for all the eggs in China.

We were half disappointed and half relieved to be told to wait outside the gate, while my father sought out his victim. There soon followed a loud cackling, raising in an hysterical crescendo and staccato beating of wings. My father reappeared, his face and hands scratched and a tiny white feather clinging to his beard, Cobra in pursuit, his long neck stretched to the limit, cackling insanely. My father dived through the gate which I had speedily opened for him, and slammed it shut on an enraged bundle of beak and claws and beating wings.

'He's too strong for me,' my father muttered. 'I'll have to do it another way. Arm yourselves with sticks. I'll fetch a rope!'

The deed was done. Cornered at last, and finally lassoed, his legs trussed, my father administered the coup de grâce. Cobra was no more. The hens, which had been running around hysterically, one laying an egg on the ground, calmed down.

But Cobra gave us one last battle. His flesh was so stringy and tough it was inedible and as he was consigned to the dustbin of history, my mother opened a can of corned beef.

None of us could meet the gaze of the others. It was as though a family member had been murdered.

Some nights in a place and time far away, I awaken suddenly, thinking I heard him crow. And my mind wanders back to see a small boy picking out bones and pieces of flesh from the dustbin, and, unknown to the family, burying them in a now forgotten corner of the hen run. He deserved this one last show of respect. He was truly a king of birds. Rest in peace, Cobra.

BIG BILLY MacGREGOR

Nicola More

HE WAS NOT A big man, but they called him Big Billy all the same. A wild-haired, wee upstart, he had sharp little eyes and a still sharper tongue. His keen sense of justice was equaled only by his keen taste for rum, and he was most often to be found making his fragrant way homeward from a session in the Crown Bar. You might call him one of life's chancers, but to most he was just Big Billy, skipper on *The Enterprise*.

Wick in those days was the largest herring port in Europe, and if you were venturing northwards your nose would pick up the trail long before the little estuary town, christened 'Vik' by the Vikings, became visible on the horizon.

Clinging to the cliffs on the north east coast, Wick enjoyed the Caithness climate of stinging gales and horizontal rain, made all the sharper by the flat lie of the land. Sunshine it may have little of, and civilisation had not yet advanced that far north, but Wick had its 'silver darlings'. The silver darlings (or herring to give it its Sunday name) were landed by the thousand, and the harbour was thronging with drifters, much to the delight of local bairns who would race from one end of the water to the other jumping from slippery deck to slippery deck.

The local spirit was one of ruthless craic and the pace of life somnambulant, but a big catch propelled the wee town into a blur of activity. Quick, slick, efficient, they lined up factory-style, women and girls of all ages, and salted and barreled the squirming flashes of silver that lit up the cool Caithness morning.

The harbour was the heart of the town, and herring its lifeblood. It was tiresome work, long and dangerous, and the memory of 'Black Saturday' lingered. A tragic story handed down through generations, of the storm that claimed the lives of 94 men. But like the miners south of the border, 'You pays your money and you takes your chances', for a living has to be made.

And so it was that Big Billy found himself one Friday afternoon being shaken like a bee in a bottle about the boat. Wave after wave lifted *The Enterprise*, and her sturdy frame battered about full of sea foam, gasping fish and shouting men. They were skilled seamen, that's for sure, but the North Sea was one of the cruellest, and on this day it seemed the gods had chosen to demonstrate their full mighty force on the little fishing boat, to the awe-struck horror of all who sailed in her. The youngest, George, was barely 18. The eldest, Big Billy himself, pushing 50. The fear took every man, young and old, as they gripped the ropes till their hands fair bled, and battled to steer their beloved vessel away from the rocky shoreline.

It's at times like these that men turn to their leader for direction, for saviour or just for comfort and reassurance. A splenetic wee man, Big Billy was not in the habit of making eloquent speeches. This was not the man who would comfort the passengers of the *Titanic* with a well-chosen sermon, far less incite them to prayer. Instead, Big Billy's mind was preoccupied by the memory of a fat, lipsticked fishwife who had told his fortune only three months hence. He had taken an instant dislike to the gypsy, with her gold rings wedged onto pudgy fingers and eyes that bulged from her head, pale and insipid like the rancid water they flung from the herring buckets each night. It seemed the feeling was mutual, for it took Margaret mere seconds to foretell Big Billy's grisly death.

'I see death for you, and soon,' she had told him in an affected, rasping voice. 'You, Big Billy, will die with your boots on.'

Well it's queer the things that will run through your head when you think death has come for you, and it was the gaping eyes of this gypsy woman who came to Billy now, while his men contemplated their fate. Throwing himself to the deck, he quickly removed his boots and stood before his crew in his stockinged soles. 'Well boys,' he said, 'if we're all going to die I'll be buggered if I'll prove that old boot right.' Gradually, the clouds cleared and the relieved men made their weary trip home.

Imagine the insult they felt on mooring at Wick Harbour to be offered half the going rate for their catch by 'Doom & Gloom', the miserable fish merchant whose greed kept a low price among fishermen too fear'd not to compete for trade. Big Billy had had enough – that day had stolen his last reserve of diplomacy – and he told 'Doom & Gloom' to go boil his head.

The fishwives say his men's wages came from his own pocket until a fair price was finally agreed, though Billy did not confirm the rumour. Still, word spread fast as the wind, as it tends to do in wee towns, and the herring girls made merry shouting, 'Here comes Wick's answer to Rob Roy,' as Billy went about his business.

He made them wince with a few choice words of a four letter description, but had a secret smile to himself at home and fancied he could well be a descendent of Red MacGregor.

On one cold, November night our hero was to be found blazing drunk at the bottom of Harbour Hill, having collapsed face down in a puddle and forgotten the use of his legs. Recognising Big Billy/ Rob Roy himself two concerned laddies grabbed him under the arms and proceeded to try to pull him to his feet, whereupon he flailed about in the murky water crying, 'Women and children first!'

And so we have my great grandfather, Big Billy: fish hustler; gypsy hater; defender of the common man; local legend and drunken lout.

WHAT KATE DID NEXT...

Lorraine Wilson

MY GRANNY, Kate Rafferty, never met the Queen, never went to the moon, never came up with a world-changing invention – she worked in the jute mills and raised a family in Midcraigie, Dundee. I was three weeks old when she died. So, to me, she is a legend.

Kate Rafferty 1893–1966

Kate was determined to find the bloody cat before the next air raid siren.

Shoving her sleeves back over substantial forearms, long past caring that the figure of her adventurous youth had gone – well, Rita Hayworth wouldn't be much good in a jute mill, would she? – Kate threw her broad back into opening the heavy sash window.

'Aw jeezy peeps! Pat! Have you pehnted this windee shut ya daftie...' After a few good heaves it was open, and Kate's tur-banned napper was dropping a good load of Woodbine ash on the pavement below.

'Hitler!!! Hitler! Whaur are yi, yi wee shite? Git in here!'

Slowly and deliberately, a sleek white tom cat with a small, but easily distinguishable jet black marking under his nose, sauntered into the closie.

'Mary! Let the cat in eh? While yir thair, mak shair yir brither's up... he's on thi back shift thi day, no' thi night shift. Eh'm needin' to git riddy fur mih spooky meetin' thi night – canna be wastin' time on a big, daft laddie.'

Kate clasped her hands together under her chin and surveyed the room. Shift the table to the middle and move the couches to the outside. Get the fire going and turn the lights down. Her 'spooky meetings' were legendary – there were seven coming tonight but there was a long waiting list. Mrs Fenwick had just lost her boy in a Japanese POW camp, so she'd be looking for results. Kate was particularly chuffed that she had managed to wangle a decent ham bone from the butcher for her pot of soup – everybody knew that favours for Kate were never forgotten.

'Muuuuummmm!!!' her youngest, Ella, wailed from the front door. 'It's Mrs Ritchie.'

Kate feared the worst. She knew that Mr Ritchie had been confined to bed for months now. She picked up a bag from the sideboard and moved quickly to the door. The anguish on Moira Ritchie's face showed her instincts were spot on. 'Come on hen, let's see ti yir man,' she said, gently placing a comforting arm around her freshly widowed neighbour's shoulders.

'Ella, tell Mary and yir daft brither ti help themselves ti soup fur tea. Eh'll be back in a wee whiley.'

'The good soup or the kale soup?' Ella pleaded.

'Gie them thi kale, but you sneak a wee bitty ham hen.' She winked at her youngest and recurled one of Ella's flagging ringlets around a strong finger.

The bag was no handbag. This was Kate's toolkit of cloths, cleansers and ointments. When someone died, the bereaved came to Kate to prepare the body for the arrival of the undertaker – at once nurse and bereavement counsellor. She had a devout faith that the grieving family would be reconciled with their loved one – not a faith that lent itself to getting out of bed for Mass on a Sunday – 'Dinna be bloody daft. If he rested on the seventh day, so will eh!' – but it was a true belief in the goodness of God, and more importantly, the strength of the family.

When you had seen as many bairns come into the world as Kate – she also happened to be Midcraigie's emergency 'midwife' – the miracle of life could not be denied. That faith was sorely tested when those worlds collided and she prepared a newborn's tiny body shortly following a stillbirth. She had experienced those herself. But only two, compared to some she knew she was lucky having four bairns left, Peter was away fighting but, ach, he would be back... eh?

It was a short walk back from Moira's but she managed to plan the table for the night's meeting. Mrs Fenwick would need to be next to her – she would need looking after more than the rest. Mrs Moran – oh jeezy peeps, nice wummin, but reekin' o' chaip perfume. She would be as far away from Kate as possible.

'Is James awa' yet?' she shouted to no-one in particular as she came back through the front door.

'He left wi' Dad,' Mary said.

'Yir dad's no' due awa' yit. Ken sumhin', I think he's got a wummin in that boatyaird...'

In reality, Patrick Rafferty had left to enjoy a couple of hours of quiet before heading to his shift at Caledon Shipbuilders. On Balgay Hill, he would roll a cigarette and look out over the industrious city. At home Kate's women would be arriving and not being an expert in small talk (as well as thinking they were all aff their bloody haids), he'd rather miss out on that.

They arrived on the dot of seven, freshly pressed in hats, coats, handbags and Sunday shoes – well when Kate connected them with their loved ones in the spirit world they'd have to be looking their best.

Full of Midcraigie gossip and soup (marvelling at the ham) they settled at the table. Kate threw back her head. 'Are yi there friend? Are yi there... Ella, come oot fae under the tabul... nothing to be scared o'. Thi spirits are oor friends. They mean us nae herm.'

As her breathing became more laboured, the atmosphere in the room changed and each of the women leaned forward hanging on every half-syllable and gasp.

After what seemed like endless minutes of silence, a tear rolled down Kate's cheek. 'Peter, that's no' you son, is it?'

Legendary Love

UNFORGETTABLE

Katie McInnes

N 1941, JIMMY WRIGHT was the tender age of 17. He was living with his family in Glasgow and he decided he wanted to join the Royal Air Force, so he lied and said he was 18. He was posted to Troon where he spent a lot of his time sailing from Ailsa Craig, Lady Isle, Arran and Troon Harbour with the Marine Craft Section.

Jimmy loved Troon, especially going to the dancing most nights in the local Town Hall. It was the winter of 1941 at the dancing that he first set eyes on my mum, Ina Morrison.

My mum was 18 in the winter of 1941, one of five sisters and one brother. My mum Ina and her sisters worked in Troon Hosiery making socks for the boys in the Forces. They worked hard and times were hard: the war rationing, the black-outs and many friends away to war.

Every night my mum, brother and sisters walked arm in arm, giggling their way through the black-out to go to the 'dancin'. All the hard times floated away when the music struck up and they took to the dance floor. Ina loved dancin' and many commented, saying she was a 'smashin' wee dancer'.

My mum and her brother Roddy were dance partners and practiced all the dances, tango, rumba, samba, foxtrot, quickstep, jitterbug etc in the kitchen at home before they 'hit the dancin''.

On a cold winter's night in 1941, Jimmy stood under the clock at the Town Hall. He was watching Ina dancing with Roddy and he thought: 'that's the girl for me'. He plucked up the courage to ask her to dance. He told me later that he felt like the luckiest man on earth when she let him walk her home, and so began a great love story.

They courted for more than a year, dancing the nights away having great fun, sharing lots of laughs and good times together, spending time with both of their families, who were growing very fond of Ina and Jimmy.

They loved the Ballast Bank area of Troon, where they often strolled hand in hand, making plans for their future.

Then, one fateful morning, the letter both had been dreading finally arrived for Jimmy. He was being called up to Burma to serve

in the war. Ina spent her last weekend with Jimmy in Glasgow. H
kissed and waved her goodbye as she left on the train from Glasgo
Central alone, not knowing if she would ever see her first love agai

Jimmy and Ina wrote to each other over the weeks and month
that followed, missing each other terribly. Jimmy's regiment fleete
across various locations throughout the globe as the war raged o
Sadly, their love letters began to go missing and eventually bot
lost touch with each other.

Jimmy was badly burned in warfare during this time, spendin
a long period of time in hospital. The months passed into years, wit
out any contact, both moving on with their lives. In the years tha
then passed both Ina and Jimmy went on to have happy marriage

Ina married my dad, Phil, a wonderful husband and fathe
Jimmy married a lovely Geordie lass, Ellen. In 1957 Jimmy, Ellen an
family emigrated to Canada. Both had children and grandchildre
and were dedicated to their families. Sadly, my dad passed away i
1986 and Jimmy's wife died in 2003.

After Jimmy's wife died, he went to live with his daughter Lynn
He told Lynne about his love for my mum. He told her that althoug
he loved his wife dearly, he had never forgotten his first love, In
Morrison.

I can remember as a child asking my mum who the handsom
man was with the lovely smile in the family album. She told me a
about Jimmy and the wonderful times they had together during th
war. She often spoke about him throughout the years.

Lynne was so touched by the story, she decided to place a
advert in the *Troon Times* headed: 'In search of Ina Morrison'. C
course she didn't know if my mum still lived in Troon or indeed if sh
was still alive as both Jimmy and Ina were now both in their 80s

My mum's neighbour saw the advert in the paper. She told m
mum about it in the local shop. It came as a huge surprise for m
mum. She told me she would love to get in touch with Jimmy agai
her first love, after 60 years of being apart. Jimmy thought my mu
was 'unforgettable' and as it turned out, he was unforgettable to

I emailed Jimmy's daughter, Lynne, and with great excitemen
we arranged for Ina and Jimmy to talk over the phone, arrangin
a special reunion. Jimmy soon left Canada to fly back to his nativ
Glasgow, making his way back to his beloved Ina in Troon.

Soon after his homecoming they strolled or should I say 'dance down memory lane, recalling their dancing days in the Town Hall 60 years ago. They were able to spend precious time together revisiting their favourite places. Both of them adored the view of Lady Isle and Arran.

Following the first visit, they talked to each other every night from Canada on the phone. Jimmy made several journeys back to Troon over the following four years. Ina and Jimmy regularly dined out and once again danced together, went lovely holidays together, took a trip on the *Waverley* around Ailsa Craig and along the coastline they both loved so much.

I remember he bought her two dozen red roses for their first Valentine's Day together during these years.

Me and the rest of the family were privileged to get to know Jimmy. He was a wonderfully colourful character. We all shared memorable times together.

Sadly, Jimmy passed away in 2008 not long after his last visit to Troon. My mum misses him so much.

It was Jimmy's last wishes to have his children and grand-children 'take him home' to scatter his ashes near the Lady Isle. And so they did. Many of the Wright clan made it over from Canada. Both 'clans' met at Troon Harbour and boarded a boat bound for Lady Isle with Jimmy's ashes. We scattered them close to the Isle. We each threw a red rose into the sea and had a 'wee dram', raising our glasses in loving memory of Jimmy Wright.

Both sides of the families keep in touch. His daughter Lynne and granddaughter Rachel will visit Scotland in April this year and will visit my mum. I know Jimmy would like that.

I so love telling this 'true love' story to friends and strangers alike. I can see in their faces just how much they enjoy it. Hope you enjoy reading this too.

OUR ROCK

Rita Dalgleish

HE WAS BORN on 30 June 1973, premature, in Cresswell, Dumfries
It was a traumatic birth, our only child. Brought up in a dysfunctiona
family, he is now a very mature, well-liked young man and quite th
rock we stand on.

I always knew I was having a boy called John (no scans then) a
soon as I knew I was pregnant. My wee precious gave new meanin
to life, a love I would never otherwise have known.

He has a mixture of dependency and independence. A fierc
loyalty to those he cares for. A disconcerting indifference to thos
who cause needless pain to himself or others (except his dad – that'
unconditional love).

J.D. taught us more than we taught him. I was far from th
perfect mum but then his dad was further from the perfec
husband. His dad is terminally ill. I have short-term memory los
due to a head injury. J.D. has met all our needs from many source
and this took a very long time. He also looks after Leah, ou
Doberman.

J.D. has not had an easy life, but he has had many wonderfu
experiences which have left their mark on his personality. Achieve
ments that only come once in a lifetime. We are so proud of him
our rock. Just look for good in all things. What did I do to deserv
such blessing?

BONNET OVER THE SNOW

Keith Ferguson

'AWAY NEXT DOOR an' mak' sure your granny's all right. Take the lamp and give her this wee drop of milk.'

The cottage was only a few snowy steps away from Elrick farmhouse, at the south end of the Cabrach, but the girl was shivering from the cold by the time she opened the cottage door. Peering into the dim light she could see her grandmother hunched up in bed, her eyes as bright as ever. She gave the old woman the milk and busied herself stirring the dying embers of the fire with some of the precious remaining logs, then tucked the blankets securely round the frail body.

'Sit by me for a few minutes, lassie,' said her grandmother.

'Now that he's dead and buried I want to speak about your grandpa.'

She paused, looking into the distance amongst the dancing shadows cast by the firelight.

'You've just known him as an auld man. You should have known him in his prime.'

'Tell me how you first met,' said the girl.

From the depths of the bed came a chuckle.

'You won't have heard of our dreadful sins. Nobody speaks about that these days. It was 1843 that John and I were hauled up afore the Kirk Session. We had to confess to the Minister and elders that we'd lain together and promise to behave ourselves in future. We got off wi' a reprimand. And the result of that was your Auntie Jane.'

'Was that when you got married then?'

'Oh, no. The good Lord kens that John and I wanted to. We loved each other. But my father wouldn't have it. He was wild. You've got to mind that he was Lieutenant James Taylor, 'The Offisher' folk called him, well in wi' the big ones in the castle, veteran o' the French Wars. And my mother? She was fair affronted, brought up in Aberdeen to be a real lady. They wouldn't have John Simpson as a son-in-law, no' sure who his father was, no land, just doing odd jobs around the crofts.'

'That still doesn't tell me how you met,' replied the girl.

A log in the fire spluttered and spat sparks over the room. B
their light the old lady's eyes gleamed.

'The Cabrach wasn't like it is today. There would be two thousand
folk at the annual fair in my young day. Today there wouldn't b
two hundred. There were ceilidhs and dances and entertainments
Your grandpa and I kept meeting and syne we fell for each other.

'Did you go on seeing him after Jane was born?'

'I didn't dare to for years. It tore the heart out of me. And the
it became too much and we got together again. So in 1848 we wer
up before the Kirk Session again, your Uncle James was on the way
confessing our sins, swearing repentance and all the rest. Anothe
reprimand. They'd have come down a lot harder on us if we hadn'
promised to get married later the same day.'

'So your father gave his consent this time?'

'Aye, well, he saw there was nothing else for it. The scandal o
having two children born out o' wedlock would have been too
much. Give him his due, he used his influence to get John the leas
of Elrick and 10 acres.'

'But the farm is much bigger than 10 acres.'

'Aye, and I wish my father had lived to see the sheer grinding
toil my John put into making the Elrick what it is today. As the
family grew – James, Alexander, William, John and your dad, Pete
forbye Jane our first, he broke in more and more of the hillside
every year with his bare hands, tearing out the gorse and heathe
heaving rocks to the side to make dykes, draining the land to make
pasture for the sheep and ground to grow their feed. Every census he
had to work out how much land he had, 10 acres at first, then 20
then 40 and so on as the family grew until he was named as 'farmer
of 80 acres'. Syne he retired and handed over the reins to your dad.

She sighed. 'Aye, he was some man, the auld breed. Nothing
would daunt him. That was why he went out these 10 days since
the snow falling like a blanket, to get food from Howbog. Eighty
I told him no' to be daft at his age, but he said your dad wa
exhausted getting the sheep in by and fed. He'd aye looked afte
me and the family and he wasn't for stopping now. It was a fearfu
shock to be told he was lost and worse to be told he was dead
That's all I remember about it. Tell me, lass, how he was found.'

The young girl wiped the tears from her eyes and tried to contro
her voice.

'We knew something was wrong, Granny, when the dog came back, but there was no hope to find him with the snow as deep as it was. When it melted days later the men found him. He hadn't got far on the road to Howbog. He was kneeling as if he was praying. His stick was planted alongside him with his bonnet on top, and that was all they saw at first.'

The old woman grasped the girl's hands.

'Thank you lassie. Now I can picture him. Let me sleep.'

It was 9am the following morning and barely light, as the girl pushed open the cottage door.

She had never seen death before but knew instantly. Her grandmother lay with her eyes closed and arms crossed in a peaceful stillness.

My wife Jean is great granddaughter of Alexander and Jane Simpson.

Alexander's death is recorded as 24/25 January 1895, the basic facts of the legend being included in a copy of the report to the procurator fiscal attached to the certificate. Jane's death is recorded as between 9pm and 9am of 3/4 February 1895.

THE KNITTER

John Mallaghan

IT WAS ONE of the coldest nights so far, of what had already been a freezing winter. There was a happy, plump-faced, full moon and the snow was falling outside in that way where it seemed to be suspended, just floating in the air, too light to bother itself with something as insignificant as gravity. The night was lit with a kind of low, eerie glow that made it feel more like late afternoon. Everyone else was in bed, but Johnnie was on his chair reading a book and gently puffing on the end of his pipe. There was still plenty of life left in the fire, and Maggie came in from the kitchen and snuggled into her chair – hers because it was in the warmest position in the room. She lifted one ball of wool from a neat pile of different colours sitting by her side, took the knitting needles propped against the chair and without any pause for thought started casting on the stitches for her latest masterpiece.

Johnnie looked over. The start was the bit that fascinated him. It always looked the same, no matter what the outcome. A simple row of stitches appeared on one needle, with no way of predicting what they would grow into. He never once asked her of course; that would have been too easy. As he watched the thick, light brown wool fill up the whole length of the left-hand needle, he couldn't help but marvel at Maggie. He was supposed to be the creative one, the one who could put his hand to anything. Music, art, poetry – you name it, Johnnie's the man! But he was in awe of Maggie's knitting. He had tried it once when he was in on his own, and finished by ripping out the bedraggled stitches less than halfway into the cast-on, silently cursing under his breath. And there she was, fingers a blur as she eased into her next creation on autopilot.

'So what is it going to be? It's surely too wide for socks,' he thought to himself.

He soon settled for a cardigan.

'Maybe it's for me – it looks like my colours.'

Johnnie sat puffing his pipe, half staring at Maggie and half staring past her, just thinking. As she moved on through the rows, seamlessly blending new colours with the original brown, her mind wandered off as usual, just sailing through the wee things she had been thinking about lately. Her thoughts shared the same space in the room as Johnnie's, oblivious to each other's existence, suspended in the air like the snowflakes outside.

Johnnie's mind started to flood with a jumble of pictures from the past, with no logic acting as the riverbank to guide the flow. The good times in the Home Guard; some of the great laughs he had had with the miners; long walks with his dad down in Thankerton; meeting Maggie; reading great books; playing the accordion; painting, and writing his poems. Other thoughts were fighting their way in there too; things he couldn't recall quite so well. Some things that hadn't happened yet, but maybe they might happen sometime in the future. Lots of children, in their own houses; they looked like bought houses too. Maggie was there, still looking great but a lot older and still helping people. And there was more music, and painting, and poetry.

Johnnie was still staring over at Maggie, on her tenth row at least by now, when his imagination started to run riot, as the fire crackled and the sparks danced up into the pitch black void of the chimney. It seemed as if Maggie's knitting had started to make sense out of his jumbled thoughts. This wasn't a cardigan anymore. It was as if the wool had become all of the strands of his life, and those lifelines, not amounting to much but full of potential, were forming into something much more worthwhile, and much more beautiful, after they had been given a new form with the knitting needles. He knew he needed somebody like Maggie to help him make sense of his life, and to help turn it into something better than it would have been, if it had been left to exist on its own.

He wanted to leap to his feet, knowing exactly how Archimedes must have felt in his bath when he had his 'Eureka!' moment. The stillness of the night and the atmosphere in the room made him think again, and he quietly reached down to the side of his chair, fumbling around for the pen and notepad he always kept there.

'What are you looking for Johnnie?'

'Oh it's fine. I just want to write something down.'

'A shopping list?'

'No Maggie, it's more like a knitting pattern.'

'Och. You can be a funny one sometimes.' She looked down and carried on with her knitting.

Johnnie thought for a few seconds, and scribbled a few words down on a new page.

February 14, 1952. Poem. 'The Knitter'.

He stared over at Maggie for a few more minutes, lightly tapping the pencil on his chin, and then wrote some more words.

Last two lines: 'And she with some infernal magic rife, Entwined her needles with my passing life.'

He liked that. And he liked the thought too. It wasn't fate that guided you. It may not even be God, although he would keep an open mind on that one, just in case. It was the lifelines of good people crossing, coming together and adding up to something even more worthwhile, then passing that something on down the line.

'Even Darwin would have appreciated that one,' he thought.

Johnnie put down the notepad and smiled, thinking he would finish the poem later, after a wee puff, or maybe in a few days, or a few weeks, whenever his mind next told him it was ready.

'I bet that is a cardigan she's knitting for me,' he thought.

INDEX

To find out about how you can get involved
in Scottish Book Trust's reading and writing projects
visit **www.scottishbooktrust.com**

Some other books published by **LUATH** PRESS

The Book That Changed My Life

Various contributors, including
Alexander McCall Smith, Janice
Galloway and Brian Cox

ISBN 978 1906817 30 5 PBK £6.99

The Book That Changed My Life
is a collection of stories from
people all over Scotland about
the books that have made an
impact on their lives.

The stories were collected by
Scottish Book Trust as part of
a project to inspire people to
talk about books. This selection
showcases the most inspirational,
touching and interesting of these
stories, including stories by
Alan Bissett, Brian Cox, Janice
Galloway, A.L. Kennedy, Kenny
Logan, Ewan Morrison, Michael
Rosen and Alexander McCall
Smith. Find out how books such
as *Lassie* or *A Clockwork Orange*
or even *101 Essential Golf Tips*
have transformed lives.

The stories contained within this
book will inspire you to look at
books differently, to read a book
you never thought you'd like and
to share your reading experiences
with other readers.

Who knows, one of these books
might just change your life too...

Days Like This: A portrait of Scotland through the stories of its people

Various contributors, including Irvine Welsh, Roddy Woomble and Hardeep Singh Kohli

ISBN 978 1906307 97 4 PBK £6.99

We all have days we'll never forget...

Days Like This is a collection of selected stories submitted by people all over Scotland as part of a national project run by Scottish Book Trust and BBC Radio Scotland.

Whether humorous, poignant, dark or surreal, the stories reveal the emotions and dramas at the heart of all human experience – a bald sixteen stone cross-dressing rugby player; a haunted pub basement; a love affair that begins outside a burning disco; a perfect day spent with a toddler – every story is unique, every one a gem.

The great thing about Days Like This *is that it simplifies and demystifies what writing is actually about. When people start from the known or the personal, it gives them the confidence to build up and then explore new issues and forms of storytelling.*

IRVINE WELSH

Luath Press Limited

committed to publishing well written books worth reading

LUATH PRESS takes its name from Robert Burns, whose little collie Luath (*Gael* swift or nimble) tripped up Jean Armour at a wedding and gave him the chance t speak to the woman who was to be his wife and the abiding love of his life. Burns called one of 'The Twa Dogs' Luath after Cuchullin's hunting dog in Ossian's *Fingal*. Luath Press was established in 1981 in the heart of Burns country, and is now based a few steps up the road from Burns' first lodgings on Edinburgh's Royal Mile.

Luath offers you distinctive writing with a hint of unexpected pleasures.

Most bookshops in the UK, the US, Canada, Australia, New Zealand and parts of Europe either carry our books in stock or can order them for you. To order direct from us, please send a £sterling cheque, postal order, international money order or your credit card details (number, address of cardholder and expiry date) to us at the address below. Please add post and packing as follows: UK – £1.00 per delivery address; overseas surface mail – £2.50 per delivery address; overseas air-mail – £3.50 for the first book to each delivery address, plus £1.00 for each additiona book by airmail to the same address. If your order is a gift, we will happily enclose you card or message at no extra charge.

Luath Press Limited
543/2 Castlehill
The Royal Mile
Edinburgh EH1 2ND
Scotland

Telephone: 0131 225 4326 (24 hours)
Fax: 0131 225 4324
email: sales@luath.co.uk
Website: www.luath.co.uk